THREADS

AND OTHER SHEFFIELD PLAYS

Edited and with an Introduction
by Michael Mangan

PAWNBROKER HOCKS THE MOON
Howard Russell

WELCOME TO THE TIMES
Dave Sheasby

THREADS
Barry Hines

Sheffield Academic Press

This collection first published in Great Britain in 1990 by Sheffield Academic Press, University of Sheffield, 343, Fulwood Road, Sheffield S10 3BP, England.

Copyright in the individual plays as follows:

Pawnbroker Hocks the Moon : copyright © 1986 by Howard Russell
Welcome to the Times: copyright © 1985 by Dave Sheasby
Threads: copyright © 1984 by Barry Hines

Copyright in this collection © 1990 by Sheffield Academic Press.

CAUTION
These plays are fully protected by copyright. Any enquiries concerning the rights for professional or amateur stage productions, broadcasting, readings, etc., should be made to:

Howard Russell: 110 Northfield Road, Sheffield S10
Dave Sheasby: c/o Michael Mangan, Department of English Literature, The University, Sheffield, S10 2TN
Barry Hines: Lemon and Durbridge Ltd, 24 Pottery Lane, Holland Park, London W11 4LZ

2·386204·21

Copyright © 1990 Sheffield Academic Press

Published by
Sheffield Academic Press Ltd
The University of Sheffield
343 Fulwood Road
Sheffield S10 3BP
England

Typeset by Sheffield Academic Press
and
printed in Great Britain
by BPCC Wheatons Ltd
Exeter

British Library Cataloguing in Publication Data

Threads and other Sheffield plays.—(Critical stages, ISSN 0953-0533; 3).
1. Drama in English, 1945- —Anthologies
I. Mangan, Michael   II. Series
822'.914'08

ISBN 1-85075-140-4

CONTENTS

General Preface · 7

Introduction · 9

PAWNBROKER HOCKS THE MOON
Howard Russell · 17

WELCOME TO THE TIMES
Dave Sheasby · 91

THREADS
Barry Hines · 157

GENERAL PREFACE

Critical Stages is based on the conviction that the last three decades have seen an extraordinary flowering of the theatre in the United Kingdom. This renaissance is comparable to the variety of output of the Elizabethan and Jacobean period. Much of this work remains unpublished, whether written for the mainstream, fringe, alternative or community theatre.

Critical Stages will publish, either in anthology or in single volumes, work which reflects the output of the last thirty years and work currently in progress. It will include plays (often early) by now established writers, work by new dramatists, television and radio scripts, plays by particular theatre companies, work developed at particular theatres, and adaptations and translations.

John Bull
Frances Gray
Michael Mangan
Philip Roberts
Theatre Workshop, Department of English Literature,
University of Sheffield, S10 2TN

INTRODUCTION

The three plays in this volume are set in the city of Sheffield. All three writers are Sheffield-based, and to that extent it is hardly surprising that they use the city as a backdrop for their stories. But in fact it is more than just a backdrop: in each of these texts the city and its particular characteristics play an important part in the narrative. But if they all take as their starting point an image of Sheffield as it used to be—producer of cutlery, high-grade steel, armaments and so on—they all, too, reflect the sense of a place in change, in turmoil, and in crisis.

Stage, screen and radio; past, present and future. Howard Russell's stage play *Pawnbroker Hocks the Moon* shows a Sheffield still on the rise, building up to one of its finest hours as a centre of munitions production in the thirties and forties. More locally, it shows a series of changes to the fabric of the social structure amongst a group of young people during the mid-thirties. The characters are all based in and around the city's steel industry: Duncan, whose father owns the steelworks which he inherits in the course of the play, is in many ways at the centre of the story. Other characters are seen in the light of their relationship to him. There is Alex, whom he will court and then marry; Rob, who is his boyhood pal, now unemployed; Michael, his works foreman; and Michael's sister Connie, whom we first meet on Duncan's arm at the Coronation Day parade. Duncan, too, is the main mover behind events in the play, and we see the direction in which he is moving in the very first scene:

ROB   Won't yer dad gi' us a job?

DUNCAN   No vacancies.

Duncan and Rob have different visions of the way the world works. Rob's question belongs to a past that is partly the world of their boyhood friendship, and partly an outdated (and perhaps illusory) notion of community loyalties. His sense of the class structure is solid enough, but couched in terms of duties and responsibilities which are almost feudal. Duncan has rejected all this: he sees himself as the new man in this world, the efficient pragmatist in a world dominated by market forces, not by sentiment. Yet his rejection has cost him, and the mantle of 'Boss' sits uneasily on his shoulders: to a great extent he yearns for a lost cameraderie, for the 'Sat'dy nights. A few bevvies dahn the boozer, fish 'n chips on the way back, then talk politics in front a' the fire. Set the world to rights'. But what the play clearly shows is that he has left all this behind him. Time and again Duncan makes decisions which consolidate his position as outsider and as Boss: it is his sense of direction which does most to break up the relationships between the various characters in the play. The first thing he does is to steal Rob's girlfriend Alex. Disillusioned and still unemployed, Rob goes off to try to find work as a builder in Spain. There, an innocent bystander, he is injured during a skirmish in the Civil War.

Between Duncan and Michael the personal and political antagonism is fiercer, for Michael too harks back to a past which he remembers as a more humane era of relationships between bosses and workers. Michael, however, is the activist, and his disgust with Duncan's restructuring of the family business into a munitions industry leads to him calling the workers out on strike. Breaking that strike, Duncan has Michael beaten and imprisoned—and Michael too leaves for Spain, but as a fighter, not a worker. Alex puts it most succinctly:

> If you hadn't've decided on me, Robby'd never have gone. If you hadn't've had Michael purrin prison he would never have gone. Do ya never think abaht the consequences?

It is a play about people growing up and changing, and getting things wrong. In a way it is Alex who gets things most wrong but who also learns most. Initially attracted to Duncan because of his power and position, she revels at first in the role of the 'power behind the throne'— urging her man on, supporting him and siding with him. Finally, though, she comes to see (albeit vaguely) the cost of their success:

> A' don't feel good abaht things. Something's not right. A' get nightmares, an' faces in the fire. They say it's hell where Michael is. Wonder what hell's like. Where all the fires 'n flames were born. P'raps ya finally get to meet some of the people whose lives so nearly touched on yours but didn't properly. Eh, worrif ya turned aht to be the best a pals? An'

that people ya thought wor enemies becomes friends an' the other way round. An' that really, everthin' wor opposite to the way it is 'ere. Bonny an' blithe an' good an' gay, instead a monstrous.

This is the nearest any character in the play comes to articulating fully the sense of loss brought on by change. But the same note is struck in an exchange which takes place in the first scene of the play:

ALEX   You'll mebbe find this hard to believe, Connie, but once upon a time. . .

DUNCAN   We wor all the best a pals.

ALEX   Churchgoers together, sang in the choir, socialised.

ROB   Different nah.

In the play's last scene—by which time things have changed even more—this exchange is repeated, but with different speakers. It marks the continuing sense of change and loss which is the central theme of the play.

In Dave Sheasby's radio play, *Welcome to the Times*, the city appears in disguise—yet the unnamed northern steel town which is the setting of this political thriller is still recognizably Sheffield. Sheasby's play, like Russell's, sets the old in conflict with the new. In this case the old is represented by an old-time left-wing Council leader, Slatterthwaite, a decent, hard-line sceptic with an unwavering faith in municipal socialism. The new is personified by the self-made opportunist Dawlish—a shady and successful entrepreneur who is looking for some dirt to use against Slatterthwaite in order to secure for himself a lucrative contract. Acting as uneasy agent for Dawlish is Fledge, ex-steelworker turned odd-job man, who reluctantly finds himself raking up muck with which to blackmail his former friend, Slatterthwaite.

The story is set against the background of a city in decline:

The city first, sullen, grey, widowed in the November rain, crisp as lace in May sunshine, empty as an echo on Sundays and at night sharp as a razor and sometimes dangerous. Cupped in hills this city and fed by tumbling rivers which race down from the purple fringe of moorland into its black heart. . . The city first, and the people. People like me. Fledge.

> A local name. Two hundred years old, they reckon, father's father, back to the early mills and forges, a long line of craftsmen down the years to this sudden, vicious full stop. Out of work, jobless, redundant, scrapped.

This is the high-redundancy modern city of silent factories and empty workshops. Sheasby's play is peopled by characters who can remember what it was like to have skilled jobs in the steel industry, and who are now trying to come to grips with the present. People like Fledge. And people like Joe, who now goes door-to-door with a pocket-sized grinding wheel, sharpening scissors for housewives and offering them his hair to test the sharpened scissors on. People like Duggie Richards, now employed as doorman at Dawlish's nightclub.

> There were two hundred and forty others wanted it... You know how I clinched it, the job? I lay on the floor at the interview and told the boss he could put his boot on my face...

And even people like Dawlish himself, whose ruthless business empire was built on a desire to escape from that very world whose passing Fledge mourns.

> I was born in Cartwright Street... So near the works, the furnace kept the house warm... My old man was at Baker and Slackleys... The old boy worked there all his life, stayed poor but loyal, got sick and died.

The city that Sheasby portrays is one in which the old patterns have already been eroded and replaced by options set by people like Dawlish and his South African business friends: sell yourself or starve. Slatterthwaite is the man that Dawlish cannot buy, so Fledge's job is to find the chink in his armour.

In both Sheasby's play and in Russell's the past is a touchstone: not because it is imagined as having been idyllic, but because the characters continually refer to times when things in general were better than they are in the present. In Barry Hines's file *Threads*, the touchstone is not the past but the present, for the change envisaged here is the most horrendous, the most cataclysmic of all. Sheffield in a possible and terrifying future is the subject of the film. It is a future whose roots are based firmly in the present, for it concerns the likely effects of a nuclear strike on the UK. The backdrop to *Threads* is the growing international tension between NATO allies and Eastern bloc countries, focussing on a conflict in the Middle East. Against this is told the story of Jimmy and Ruth—two young people in their early twenties. Their story, to start off with, is told in a style reminiscent of an old 'Play for Today': social issues presented as social realism. The couple are courting; Ruth gets accidentally pregnant; they decide to keep the baby and get married; they buy a flat and are well on their way to a qualifed happy-ever-after when somebody somewhere pushes a button. One of the most memorably chilling moments of the film is the point where Jimmy and his workmate Bob stand, aghast, watching the mushroom cloud rise above the horizon: 'Jesus Christ!' says Bob, 'They've done it. They've done it.'

Threads was filmed mainly on location in Sheffield itself, with the co-operation and participation of hundreds of local people, many of them recruited through the Sheffield peace movement. It is an extraordinary, dense, powerful and bleak film. Western culture has often given itself a kind of thrill by contemplating a post-Holocaust world. Fantasy and sci-fi films like *Mad Max* portray a barbaric wasteland, peopled by the plainly good and the unspeakably bad. The landscape serves as a backdrop for stories of heroism and the 'affirmation of the human spirit' as understood by Hollywood (which is largely involves the notion of good people eventually banding together and beating hell out of the bad). Even those dramas which do not take the meretricious route of suggesting it all might be rather fun after the bomb drops, often fall prey to this tendency—or perhaps this need—to accentuate the positive and eliminate the negative: a prime example of this is the American made-for-TV blockbuster *The Day After*. *Threads* is the polar opposite of these things, and one of the factors which gives it its particular power is the way in which Hines concentrates on factual detail. The specifics of time and place are essential to the story.

This is emphasized by the variety of means with which the story is told. Cutting across the naturalism of the Jimmy-and-Ruth plot are the techniques of the drama-documentary. Newsreel footage, still photographs, voice-over commentary, captions spelling out facts and figures: all of these are central narrative techniques of the play. They are also part of the play's subject-matter. In the early part of the story, which shows the build-up to the actual nuclear strike itself, scenes between characters are played out to the constant background sound of news bulletins on radios and televisions. The presence of the media itself, continually updating, interviewing, reporting, informing and analysing the slow build-up to Armageddon is a major feature of the play. Nor is this mere self-indulgence: the starting point of *Threads* is the way in which 'in an urban society, everything connects'. These connections take place through technology, electricity, transport, the media—in fact the whole complex web of communications networks which we take for granted.

The second half of the story details the breakdown of these connections in the event of a nuclear strike. Our everyday world of daily milk deliveries, computer games and telephone calls, of radio, TV and newspapers collapses and what Hines shows, with devastating precision, is what happens once this communications network is shattered. Local Government Officers try to organize a post-nuclear survival from a bunker in the basement of the Town Hall, cut off from the rest of the world by debris which nobody can be mobilized to shift. They maintain sporadic and ever-decreasing contact with the outside world by means of nearly inaudible radios. The fragmented networks which do remain are unable even to begin to deal with the problems of the period immediately after the attack.

In this part of the film the documentary element looms ever larger. A selection from the captions and commentary gives some idea of the general tone:

> East-West exchange three thousand megatons. Two hundred and ten megatons fall on UK. Two-thirds of houses in Britain within possible fire zones...
>
> The first fallout dust settles on Sheffield. It's an hour and twenty-five minutes after the attack. An explosion on the ground at Crewe has sucked up this debris and made it radioactive...
>
> Attack plus one week. Food stores controlled by central government representatives. No food distribution likely until two weeks after attack...
>
> The entire peacetime resources of the British Health Service—even if they survived—would not be able to cope with the effects of even the single bomb that's hit Sheffield...
>
> In the grim economics of the aftermath there are two harsh realities. A survivor who can work gets more food than one who can't and the more who die, the more food is left for the rest...

In a scene from the end of the film, set ten years after the attack, children in a barn-turned-schoolroom sit dumbly and incomprehendingly in front of a salvaged video machine, powered by a home-made generator, watching the flickering remnants of a pre-Holocaust schools programme. It is a poignant and painful echo of the past, for the technology now means nothing to them. It is meaningless to them, not only because the technology is now irrelevant—little more than a museum piece which will soon wear out and cannot be replaced—but also because they themselves are losing their very ability to comprehend and interpret the mechanically reproduced image. Soon the language itself, the most basic of the 'threads' that link us together, will be in the process of disintegration. In the future that Hines depicts, survivors from pre-Holocaust times still speak our language; but those who were born or grew up after the attack have developed a dialect of their own— guttural and abbreviated, a language of survival and necessity.

And the city itself is a character which gets written out of the story. Like Jimmy, Ruth's boyfriend, who disappears and is never heard of again, the city becomes redundant as the pattern of life reverts to a medieval agrarian subsistence economy. The last stages of the film are set in desolate moorlands above and beyond the site that used to be Sheffield. The rubble of urban society is irrelevant in such times.

Each of these three plays stands on its own. Yet, taken together, they show a stark and terrifying graph of the rise and fall of an urban industrial society. Past, present and future. And meanwhile, in the real world, the city continues to change, generating new images, new self-images, and new stories.

Mick Mangan

PAWNBROKER HOCKS THE MOON

Howard Russell

This play is fully protected by copyright. Any queries concerning the rights for professional or amateur stage productions, broadcasting, readings etc., should be made to Howard Russell, 110 Northfield Road, Sheffield.

PAWNBROKER HOCKS THE MOON was commissioned and first performed by Metro Theatre Company at the Mappin Art Gallery, Sheffield, on 18 October 1986. The cast was as follows

Alex............... HEIDI GJERTSEN
Rob................NEIL GORE
Duncan............COLIN CAMPBELL
Connie............BARBARA DRYHURST
Michael...........MARK SPALDING

Directed by STEPHEN DALDRY

Scene One

> ROB, ALEX, DUNCAN and CONNIE. ROB *carries a parcel of newspapers. Crowd noises.*

ALEX   Think they' startin'?

ROB   'Eard the news? Dutch've invaded 'Olland.

DUNCAN   Didn't a' see thee robbin' litter bins dahn the Wicker?

ROB   What wor tha doin' dahn there then?

DUNCAN   I'd be workin', not shirkin'.

ROB   Tha don't know the difference.

DUNCAN   Yeh, it's all work wi' me.

ROB   Wish I'd a quid for every bar tha's propped up.

DUNCAN   What' you doin' dahn 'ere, day off?

ROB   Yore try gerrin' a job.

> *A fanfare of trumpets.* ROB *sets the newspapers down.*

ALEX   (*to* CONNIE). What's yer name love?

DUNCAN   Jealous?

ALEX   That why ya brought her?

CONNIE   Me name is Connie.

ALEX   Ya might've introduced us.

DUNCAN   (*to* ALEX). What' ya doin' Friday?

ALEX   Nothin'.

DUNCAN	Enjoy thi'sen.
ROB	Oh, an' the King's dead; him wi' the beard. Come in number five, yer time's up.
DUNCAN	Two women 'ere, squabblin' fomme favours.
ROB	Who's workin' you?
ALEX	Only a bit a fun.
DUNCAN	(*to* ALEX) Are ya not upset?
ALEX	Naow.
DUNCAN	Knew you'd be 'ere.
ALEX	Come wi' Rob.
DUNCAN	An' I come wi' Connie.
CONNIE	Is there anybody 'ere ya don't know?
DUNCAN	There's that brunette there, an' her in them high 'eels there, (*to* ALEX) an' this one 'ere—as ya wor—a' know this one very well.
CONNIE	An' d'yer friends choose you, or you them?
DUNCAN	Specially selected, so they'll not tell on us.
CONNIE	Better not.

The LORD MAYOR's *reading of the proclamation begins, over the tannoy.*

	Hu. New beginnings. Wonder what they'll bring?
ALEX	A bathroom.
DUNCAN	Romance.

DUNCAN *makes a play for* CONNIE.

CONNIE	Space.
ROB	Money.

ROB *picks* DUNCAN'S *pocket.*

CONNIE	No. Don't.

DUNCAN	Relax. Enter the new man.
ALEX	Why don't yer ever hold me like that?
DUNCAN	Safest place there is, a mob of plebs.
ROB	Wash yer mouth aht, there's a king bein' invented 'ere.
LORD MAYOR	. . . the High 'n Mighty Prince Edward, Albert, Christian, George, Andrew, Patrick, David. . .
ALEX	There'll be a shootin' star tonight.
CONNIE	Or an earthquake.
DUNCAN	Or one a Mussolini's meteorites up yer arse.
ROB	Gi' yer tongue a day off.
DUNCAN	(*to* CONNIE) Betcha don't even know where Abyssinia is.
CONNIE	A' bi' seein' ya.
	DUNCAN *and* CONNIE *kiss.*
ALEX	Worrabaht me?
ROB	Worrabaht thee?
ALEX	Kiss?
ROB	Alright, you asked for it.
	ALEX *waits for a kiss.*
DUNCAN	(*pushing* ROB *aside*). Don't be dirty.
	DUNCAN *kisses* ALEX
ROB	'Ere. . .
DUNCAN	Only playin'. Well, worrizit? Abyssinia.
CONNIE	It's a confectionary, like Madagascar.
ROB	Ignorant cow.
	CONNIE *slaps* ROB. *They all laugh.*
DUNCAN	It's a filthy hole, full a nigs 'n mosquitoes.
ROB	See.

CONNIE	A' wor jokin'.
LORD MAYOR	... the High 'n Mighty Prince Edward, Albert, Christian, George, Andrew, Patrick, David...
DUNCAN	Sydney, 'Erbert, Rod'rick, Quentin.
ROB	(*sung*). Oh, the, sun has got his hat on, hip hip hip hooray...

DUNCAN *and* ALEX *join in*

DUNCAN, ALEX, ROB	The sun has got his hat on and he's coming out today.
CONNIE	Oh God, a' knew it. Let go. Let go.
DUNCAN	Who is it?
CONNIE	Me father-in-law, he's seen me. That wor you singin'.

CONNIE *tries to push her way through the crowd*

DUNCAN	They're packed solid.
CONNIE	Everybody's watchin' me.
DUNCAN	Calm dahn, tha'll give the game away.
CONNIE	He's seen me. They've all seen me.
LORD MAYOR	... With long 'n happy years to reign over us.

Drum roll for the start of the National Anthem. ROB *stands on the pile of newspapers.*

CONNIE	God save the King.
DUNCAN	Connie.
CONNIE	Buggerit. If tha can broadcast to the world, so can I. God save the soddin' King.

ALEX *and* DUNCAN *join in the National Anthem.*

ROB	Read all abaht it. The King is dead. Taygrafaystaw. Died in his bed.

ROB *sings.*

Oh yes the King is dead
He did die in his bed

	The do-ho-cters 'n surgeons said He-e hada bad head.
LORD MAYOR	By due proclamation of law, this twenty-second day of January, in the year of Our Lord one thousand nine hundred 'n thirty-six.
ROB	To our right High 'n Mighty Liege Lord...
	ALEX *and* DUNCAN *join in with the three cheers.*
	Hip, hip, hooray. Hip, hip, hooray. Hip, hip, hooray.
	The crowd surges forward. CONNIE *falls down.*
CONNIE	Where is he?
	DUNCAN *helps* CONNIE *up.*
	Grey cap.
	ROB *cuts the string and takes out a newspaper*
DUNCAN	He's gone, he's gone.
CONNIE	Yeh, an' I know where. Straight home to tell on me.
ROB	Taygrafaystaw.
CONNIE	Can't ya do summat with him?
	A military band strikes up.
	Bloody'ellfire.
DUNCAN	I'm off. Get home on yer own.
CONNIE	Duncan, no. He hits me.
DUNCAN	Hit him back.
CONNIE	You hit him for me. Will ya? See to him for me.
DUNCAN	Nowt to do wi' me.
CONNIE	Buggeroff then.
ROB	Taygrafaystaw.
DUNCAN	Pack it in Rob, you'll gerrus locked up.
ROB	I'm tryin' to earn a livin'.

ALEX	This is last night's.
ROB	A' sell yesterday's news.
ALEX	That's dishonest.
DUNCAN	So's yesterday's news.
CONNIE	I've sprained me ankle.

CONNIE *sits on the pile of newspapers.* ROB *shoves* DUNCAN

ROB	I've got no work. What's tha gonna do abaht it?

DUNCAN *grabs* ROB'S *arm.*

Eh? Love?

DUNCAN	Get thi'sen in the army.
ROB	I've got flat feet.
DUNCAN	Tha's gorra flat 'ead.

ROB *takes a swipe at* DUNCAN.

ALEX	Don't ask me to brush the blood away.
DUNCAN	Only thi'sen to blame if tha's no job.
ROB	(*to* ALEX). Whose side'r you on?
DUNCAN	Mine. Why d'ya think she's 'ere?
ROB	That's your version.
CONNIE	You'd better gimme a lift home Duncan.
ROB	(*to* ALEX). Well?
ALEX	Yours.
ROB	A' didn't have to bring thi wimme.
ALEX	Don't bother next time.
ROB	Stay at home. Saves on the gravy brownin'.
ALEX	They' stockins.
ROB	Tek 'em off then, let's have a shufti.
CONNIE	Duncan.

DUNCAN	Hang abaht, young Robby's promised us a good dustin' dahn.
ROB	Don't think a' wouldn't.
DUNCAN	Foreign Legion needs twerps like thee. Go 'n stop the Ities in Africa.
	ROB *squares up to* DUNCAN.
CONNIE	Forgerrit, I'll crawl 'ome.
	ALEX *steps between* ROB *and* DUNCAN.
ALEX	D'you two want yer 'eads bangin' together?
	CONNIE *cries out, having tried, and failed, to get up.* ALEX *takes* DUNCAN'S *scarf off.*
	For the lady. It might be broken. Grown men.
ROB	Won't yer dad gi' us a job?
DUNCAN	No vacancies.
ALEX	Heavy words, like Sheffield soot. (*To* ROB). Scarf.
	ROB *takes his scarf off.*
	You'll mebbe find this hard to believe Connie, but once upon a time...
DUNCAN	We wor all the best a pals.
ALEX	Churchgoers together, sang in the choir, socialised.
ROB	Different nah.
DUNCAN	You are.
ROB	Tha got big-'eaded.
ALEX	Grow up, yer s'posed to be men.
DUNCAN	(*holding up a newspaper*). Is this manly?
ROB	I'll beat thee before I'm done.
DUNCAN	What with?
ROB	Not me fists. This (*Taps his forehead.*) An' tha's gorra start on me.

DUNCAN Glad ya recognise it, duckbrain.

ROB Tha's got more money.

DUNCAN Look at him, eyes poppin' aht. (*To* ALEX.) Used to share the same girlfriend, me 'n him. Unbelievable, in't it?

ROB Now tha's got her all to thi'sen.

ALEX Robby?

ROB Naw, thee mek thi bed, wha' do I care?

DUNCAN He's peeved coz me dad won't gi' him a job.

ROB A' should never meet a bigger shit than thee.

DUNCAN Me dad's lookin' for men, not dimwits.

ROB I'll bloody maim thee.

CONNIE He's slow-timin' ya Rob, can't ya see?

ROB Alright for him, gets his dad to sub him.

DUNCAN No need to, practically in charge nah.

ROB Why won't tha gimme a job then?

DUNCAN Never accept 'and-outs, it meks thi weak.
(*To* CONNIE). Come on then if tha wants a lift.

CONNIE Gonna be strong an' catch a tram.

DUNCAN Do a' tek it we'll not be goin' dahn the Pally tonight?

CONNIE Which one of us'r ya talkin' to?

CONNIE *goes off.*

DUNCAN I'll have me wallet back nah. If ya don't mind.

ROB *hands over the wallet and goes to collect his newspapers.* DUNCAN *sets off down the street.*

ALEX Duncan.

ALEX *goes up to* DUNCAN

Ah... How is yer dad? Is he any better?

DUNCAN Not so good. He'll not live long.

Scene Two

> ALEX *and* DUNCAN *approach the car.* DUNCAN *wears a black armband. He goes round the back.* ALEX *coughs.*

DUNCAN Oh, yeh.

> DUNCAN *opens the door for* ALEX.
>
> It's a Morris. Fourteen.

ALEX Sounds cheap.

DUNCAN Horse power.

ALEX Oh. Kiss?

> *They kiss.* DUNCAN *gets in the driver's seat.*
>
> You're a bit subdued.

DUNCAN Am a'?

ALEX Must be summat on yer mind, you've hardly said a word. Is it yer dad?

DUNCAN Not exactly.

ALEX Is it me?

DUNCAN Not exactly. Thought we'd go into Derbyshire.

ALEX Yeh, alright. Ya know yer summat special if ya gerra ride in Duncan Battersby's motor.

DUNCAN New car. You're the first.

ALEX An' me birthday's not till next month. The ninth.

DUNCAN Might gi' ya this.

ALEX A' might tek it.

DUNCAN So... Thought we'd have a chat.

ALEX Worrabaht?

DUNCAN Things. Bin goin' aht together now for...

ALEX Three weeks two days, must be a record.

DUNCAN	Not countin' St. James's.
ALEX	Abaht the future then.
DUNCAN	Yeh.
ALEX	Go on, start it up.

DUNCAN *starts the car*.

Very impressive.

They set off.

DUNCAN	Alright?
ALEX	Never felt better.
DUNCAN }	The reason I'm a bit quiet...
ALEX }	He musta bin very popular to have...
DUNCAN	Passengers first.
ALEX	A' wor just goin' to say, yer dad seems to've bin a well-respected man.
DUNCAN	He wor only fifty-three. Know what age I am?
ALEX	Twenty-eight on the twenty-first of August.
DUNCAN	Half me life's ovver.
ALEX	With half to come.
DUNCAN	An a' still don't know what to do with it.
ALEX	Don't ya?
DUNCAN	Not for certain.
ALEX	Thought you'd be tekin' ovver from yer dad.
DUNCAN	I always thought a' might go on expeditions to distant lands. Or play cricket for Yorkshire.
ALEX	Growin' pains.
DUNCAN	Yeh. No but, them coulda bin real opportunities for me, me dad coulda set it up: farmin', music, the Church. It wor up to me to say.

ALEX	Don't ya like mekin' 'ammers?
DUNCAN	Not the only thing we mek.
ALEX	Watch the road.
DUNCAN	Might not be mekin' anythin' for much longer. Slowly but surely runnin' ahta business. The markets'r disappearin'.
ALEX	What else can ya do?
DUNCAN	Conquer Everest, win the ashes, be a monk.
ALEX	Abaht the business.
DUNCAN	Dunno.
ALEX	Bin in the family for generations, 'ant it?
DUNCAN	Only three.
ALEX	You've a tradition to keep goin'.
	The car stalls.
DUNCAN	Damn. Ignition's cold. Might want crankin'.
	DUNCAN *gets out.*
ALEX	What wor you goin' to say?
DUNCAN	What, abaht feelin' aimless?
ALEX	Yeh.
DUNCAN	Well, a' feel aimless.
	DUNCAN *takes the crank out.*
ALEX	That why we're 'ere? Coz yer at a loose end?
DUNCAN	No.
ALEX	Why then.
DUNCAN	Test drive.
ALEX	Duncan.
DUNCAN	It's hard to say it. I'm twenty-eight next—
ALEX	A' know how old you are.

DUNCAN   So... A' thought you 'n me might... Ya know.
ALEX   Jump in the back seat an' test the springs aht?
DUNCAN   No.
ALEX   Break dahn in the country an' spend all night together?
DUNCAN   No. No.
ALEX   Why not?
DUNCAN   What?
ALEX   Why not?
DUNCAN   Well... Because.
ALEX   Because it's a compliment.
DUNCAN   Yeh.
ALEX   Call that a compliment? Not tekin' me in the back a the car?
DUNCAN   No. Yeh.
ALEX   Look, it's either a compliment or it's norra compliment.
DUNCAN   D'you wanna drive this bloody car?
ALEX   Yeh, alright then.

         ALEX *climbs into the driver's seat.*

         Learnt to drive years ago.
DUNCAN   No ya didn't.
ALEX   There wor a tractor on me uncle's farm.
DUNCAN   Yer quite a girl, aren't ya?
ALEX   I know what you need.
DUNCAN   What?
ALEX   Marriage.
DUNCAN   Everybody has a wife, sometime.
ALEX   An' ya can't get married half-way up a mountain, or chasin' a cricket ball.

DUNCAN	Dunno.
ALEX	Yer to carry on wi' yer dad's firm.
DUNCAN	Mebbe.
ALEX	What's the point in buildin' what yer dad has just to let it die with him?
DUNCAN	It'd probably mean changin' ovver to an entirely different manufacture.
ALEX	So?
DUNCAN	It's a big risk.
ALEX	I'd call it a challenge.
DUNCAN	Reckon we could do it?
ALEX	Yes. I do.
DUNCAN	Alright.
ALEX	Crank it up.

DUNCAN *turns the crank.*

Harder, do it harder.

DUNCAN *turns the crank.*

Go on, bend yer legs.

DUNCAN *turns the crank.*

Get a sweat on. Put yer body into it.

The car starts.

Perfect. Just perfect.

DUNCAN *gets into the passenger seat.*

DUNCAN	Be a shame to have to tek the notice dahn: Battersby 'n sons.
ALEX	An' daughters.
DUNCAN	Oh, yeh. But we've gorra keep the line goin'.
ALEX	So, at least one boy.

DUNCAN At least.

ALEX Just so's a' know.

DUNCAN You sure ya can drive this thing?

ALEX puts the car into first gear.

Yer a remarkable girl.

ALEX A' know what a' want.

DUNCAN Watch the road.

ALEX A' get big dreams abaht us two.

DUNCAN Oh yeh?

ALEX Grow together, protect one another, gather what's ours around us, safe.

DUNCAN Mek a good marriage, so us kids'll grow up strong an' push themselves forwards.

ALEX That's how it should be.

DUNCAN Go to the right 'ere. An' if some of 'em want to be explorers, or musicians...

ALEX S'not everybody that can mek 'ammers.

DUNCAN Or whatever we end up mekin'.

ALEX Gorra move on. How difficult will it be, switchin' ovver?

DUNCAN Everybody else is goin' into munitions.

ALEX Eh, if ya do that, when the war comes, you'll be able to stay at home: reserved occupation.

DUNCAN Well, we shall see. Watch this bend.

ALEX Which way?

DUNCAN To the right. To the right.

Scene Three

Hallway. A shopwindow mannikin modelling an arm sling, splints to the leg and a head bandage. ALEX *and* CONNIE *walk through.* ALEX *carries blankets.*

CONNIE	You've no room Alex. How'r ya gonna fit me in?
ALEX	I'll fit yer in.
CONNIE	Why should ya?
ALEX	Ya what?
CONNIE	Why are ya fittin' me in?
ALEX	Gonner help with the rent, aren't ya?
CONNIE	Yer only doin' it coz a' threatened to tell on Duncan.
ALEX	Listen. A' want this straight from the start. I like things aht in the open. Yer husband batters ya; ya need a roof ovver yer head; ya need to gerraway. Right?
CONNIE	Right.
ALEX	Well there's a plenty a room 'ere.
CONNIE	There wor nothin' between me 'n him.
ALEX	That's what he said.
CONNIE	A' wor desperate.
ALEX	Fellas. If Duncan ever hit me I'd kill him. Hard to blame them though, what with the war and the depression.
CONNIE	What's this?
ALEX	An old dummy from the shop.
CONNIE	Bandages?
ALEX	Nursin' practice for St. John's. A' don't do it now. Eh, why don't you have a go? You'd look great in a uniform.
CONNIE	I've gorra gerra job.

MICHAEL *comes in carrying baggage.*

ALEX — More?

MICHAEL — There's more yet.

ALEX — In 'ere.

ALEX and MICHAEL go out.

CONNIE — (*to the mannikin*). What happened to you?

MICHAEL comes back.

Burn the toast? Forget to iron his socks? Did ya talk back to him?

MICHAEL — Worrif it's a male?

CONNIE — Don't think so.

MICHAEL — S'got the look a your Battersby: squinty-eyed.

CONNIE — Not my Battersby.

MICHAEL — Yes, he's definitely a eunuch this one. They cut 'em off so's the girls don't get too excited when they' window-dressin'.

CONNIE — I'm not in the mood Michael.

MICHAEL — Only a joke.

CONNIE — Yeh, wish I knew some.

MICHAEL — Shall ya be alright 'ere, our kid?

CONNIE — Safer 'ere, aren't a'?

MICHAEL — Dunno. What's the situation?

CONNIE — Wha'd'ya mean?

MICHAEL — There's her 'n you, 'ere, together. There's Battersby, aht there somewhere. No doubt be callin' in, sometime. Is this his harem?

CONNIE — Oh for God's sake, stop talkin' abaht me as if I'm the dark lady in some seedy affair.

MICHAEL — Touchy.

CONNIE	Can't ya refer to me in any other way than through sex?
MICHAEL	Ya never wanted it any other way.
CONNIE	Who says?
MICHAEL	Tha wor always a scandal when it comes to boyfriends: 'Look at our Connie in her warpaint. Wonder how many braves'r gonna get shot dahn tonight?'
CONNIE	Them days'r gone.
MICHAEL	Yeh, an' they' not comin' back, not the way things'r shapin' up. You'll be right, you've gorra tough skin. Don't know abaht this one though.
CONNIE	Who?
MICHAEL	(*referring to the mannikin*). Young Battersby. Duncan Disorderly.
CONNIE	What' ya got against him?
MICHAEL	What haven't a'? Don't listen to anythin' a' say abaht Battersby an' mistek it for thee, it's guaranteed to offend.
CONNIE	Everybody calls their boss.
MICHAEL	Ah, but this one teks the biscuit.
CONNIE	He's young, gi' him a chance.
MICHAEL	It's the thought of him gerrin' older, that's what really worries me. Ya should see what he's gerrin' up to.
	ROB *walks in with a string bag full of beer bottles.*
	I'll bring the rest.
CONNIE	Rob.
	MICHAEL *goes.*
ROB	Is Alex in?
CONNIE	Yeh.
ROB	Come to see her. Duncan 'ere?

CONNIE   No. You alright?

ROB   I'm alright if you're alright.

CONNIE   I'm alright.

ALEX *comes back.*

ALEX   Nah then. Alright?

CONNIE   Kitchen

CONNIE *goes out.*

ROB   Hear tha's gerrin' wed.

ALEX   He's comin' round later.

ROB   Brung some beer.

ALEX   We' savin' the celebrations.

ROB   Who says it's for thee? Tha's not the only one wi' news.

ALEX   Oh?

ROB   Marry me an' I'll tell ya.

ALEX   Robby. A' wor always gonner end up with one a ya, burrit wor my choice, not yours. An' tha wor never forced to be the chosen one.

ROB   I'll forgive ya. I'll even forget ya. Oo, ya don't like that. The beer's coz I'm leavin' the country. Got meself a job.

ALEX   Good. I'm really pleased for ya.

ROB   The job's abroad. I'm emigratin'.

ALEX   Not the end a the world.

ROB   It's far enough. I'm goin' to the continent.

ALEX   It's time ya gi' yerself a bit of a push. You've gorra lot to offer.

ROB   Oh yeh? What? Deh. Ya can't think a nowt.

ALEX   Yerself. You.

ROB	It's a job. No job, no brass, no snap.
ALEX	Right.
ROB	He'll be 'ere soon.
ALEX	Stay. Stay 'n drink yer beer.
	ROB *puts the bag down.*
ROB	Strange job for a bloke wi' the jitters, mekin' 'ammers.
ALEX	Robby.
ROB	Bang Bang Battersby we used to call him, coz he wor jumpy. We'd stick frogs dahn his shirt an' watch him throw a corble.
ALEX	He don't mek 'ammers any more.
ROB	What's he mek?
ALEX	He's diversifyin'.
ROB	Is he? Oh, yeh, I've seen him in his suit. Course, fellas in pin-stripes run this world.
ALEX	They' not pin-stripes.
ROB	With an army a muscular women bringin' up the rear.
ALEX	I'm norra weightlifter.
ROB	Never mind, I still fancy ya.
ALEX	There's no point in this.
ROB	Don't come crawlin' back to me when ya fall off cloud nine.
ALEX	Nothin' quite so dreamy abaht me 'n him. Feet on the ground.
ROB	Avoidin' all the cracks?
ALEX	Drink yer beer.
	DUNCAN *comes in.*
	An' shek his hand when he arrives—oh, there y'are.
DUNCAN	Rob.

ROB	Duncan.
	DUNCAN *moves towards* ROB, *his hand outstretched.* ROB *steps back and knocks the mannikin over.*
ALEX	It's alright. It wain't valuable.
	CONNIE *runs in brandishing a frying-pan.*
CONNIE	What happened?
	MICHAEL *comes on with more baggage.*
MICHAEL	That's it. That's the end of it.
ALEX	Er... Duncan, this is Connie's brother, Michael.
DUNCAN	A' know Michael, he works for me.
ALEX	Oh.
MICHAEL	Mester Battersby.
CONNIE	An' this is Rob, Michael.
MICHAEL	Rob.
ROB	Michael.
	CONNNIE *starts to giggle.*
ALEX	(*to* MICHAEL) An' my name's Alex.
CONNIE	Oh I'm sorry, a' forgot to say.
MICHAEL	Alex... Rob... Mester Battersby
DUNCAN	Duncan, just for tonight.
MICHAEL	Duncan.
CONNIE	An' brother Michael.
	ALEX *starts to laugh.*
MICHAEL	Connie?
	Both women laugh.
DUNCAN	What's so funny?
ALEX	You three.

CONNIE	Starin' at one another. (*Butch voice*). Gofer yer guns kid.
ALEX	An' this place, looka the state of it.
CONNIE	Like a junk shop.
ALEX	(*to* MICHAEL) Wanna buy a dummy, guv?
CONNIE	House clearance vultures hoverin' ovver the remains.
ROB	A' don't gerrit.
ALEX	(*to* DUNCAN) There's some supper if yer hungry.
DUNCAN	Had a pork pie at the boozer.
ALEX	Rob? Michael?

CONNIE *capsizes into laughter, followed by* ALEX.

I've got to go.

CONNIE	We've got to go.

ALEX *and* CONNIE *go out.* DUNCAN *helps himself to a beer.*

ROB	Help thi'sen.
DUNCAN	Are they yours? Gorra bottle opener? Don't need one.

DUNCAN *takes the top off one with his teeth.*

There y'are.

DUNCAN *hands the bottle to* MICHAEL.

MICHAEL	Ta.

DUNCAN *takes the tops off two other bottles and hands one to* ROB.

DUNCAN	Sat'dy nights. A few bevvies dahn the boozer, fish 'n chips on the way back, then talk politics in front a the fire. Set the world to rights. That's the way it's always bin.

They drink. CONNIE *returns with beer glasses. She stands at the back.*

So. Wha'd'ya reckon to Duff Cooper?

ROB Who's he?

DUNCAN Brightest man in politics. Knows abaht practicalities.

MICHAEL A' know why yer askin' that. Coz he's all for the Territorials, an' so'r you.

DUNCAN But not our Michael.

MICHAEL Glorified boy scouts.

ROB Is he mekin' ya join the Territorials?

DUNCAN It won't hurt him. Good clean fun, healthy exercise.

ROB sings.

ROB Yer in the army now Yer not behind a plough...

DUNCAN They' volunteers, man.

ROB Makes it easier for 'em to call yer up.

DUNCAN Nobody's talkin' abaht conscription. Listen. If the Germans'd've landed a U-boat on the beach at Brid an' a hundred Krauts wi' machine-guns'd've come up the sands, what would yer've done? Tret 'em to a candyfloss apiece?

ROB If a hundred Germans can do summat wi' Bridlington, they' welcome to it.

DUNCAN I'm trying' to talk to Michael.

ROB I've gorra job now, a' can speak if a' want to.

DUNCAN Have ya?

MICHAEL Duncan, can yer explain to me what we' doin' dahn the works? All this choppin' 'n changin'.

DUNCAN Just a sec. (*To* ROB) Worrabaht them lorry drivers in Manchester? Wha'd'ya do wi' them? Let 'em do what they want?

CONNIE Are they doin' anythin' wrong?

For a moment all three men stare at CONNIE.

DUNCAN They' threatenin' to go on strike. Fotty thousand on 'em.

CONNIE	Ah, so, they haven't actually gone on strike.
DUNCAN	Who's gonner handle the goods in 'n ahta Liverpool? There'd be a log-jam all the way back to New York.
MICHAEL	Is it true? That yer turnin' the shop floor ovver to munitions?
DUNCAN	That's my business, not yours. (*To* CONNIE) How many woulda died at that benzol fire at Kilnhurst if there hadn't a bin volunteers? Eh?
CONNIE	What's that go to do wi' owt?

ALEX *brings in a plate of food.*

DUNCAN	(*to* ROB) Look at Palestine, our lads'r short-'anded. We could send more regulars aht there an' cover at 'ome wi' Territorials.
ROB	That's the last thing we want, pretend soldiers drinkin' the pubs dry.
DUNCAN	Worrabaht these drug addicts? Thirty thousand on 'em. Who's gonna clear the streets a them scabs?
ROB	Have the police gone on holiday through all this?
DUNCAN	I'll fill thee in if tha can't be serious. An' if ya can't, shut yer trap an' let others talk that can be.
ALEX	'Ere, get this dahn yer throat. That'll stop yer arguin'.

ALEX *gives the food to* DUNCAN.

Politics.

DUNCAN	Duff Cooper's alright.
ALEX	Duff?
MICHAEL	Great name for a politician.
DUNCAN	Are you a troublemaker?
MICHAEL	Duncan.
DUNCAN	An' stop callin' me Duncan. Ya sound like me mother.
MICHAEL	Can ya confirm it or not? We tek equipment aht, we bring

new equipment in. God knows where the money's comin' from.

DUNCAN A' never discuss the details wimme employes an' if a' did a' wouldn't do it 'ere.

MICHAEL It's a straightforward question.

DUNCAN *eats*.

Are ya transferrin' yer operation ovver to the war effort? Yes or no.

ALEX Duncan knows what he's abaht an' when the time comes—

MICHAEL Don't ya wanna know what yer men think?

CONNIE Michael.

DUNCAN *continues eating*.

MICHAEL (*handing his beer to* CONNIE). Finish this for us. I'm away now. G'night.

MICHAEL *leaves*.

DUNCAN (*calling after him*) An' don't be late on Monday.

ALEX Has he upset ya love?

DUNCAN Ya just can't get through to some people. There's no sauce on this.

ALEX *goes out*.

CONNIE You'll not sack him.

DUNCAN Michael's bin the best foreman me dad's ever had.

ALEX *comes back in, with sauce*.

CONNIE Wor that an answer?

DUNCAN (*to* ALEX) Are we gonna sack Michael?

ALEX Sack him?

DUNCAN He's a troublemaker.

ALEX If he's a good worker. . .

Pawnbroker Hocks the Moon

ROB *works at the top of another bottle with his teeth.*
DUNCAN *and* ALEX *talk between themselves.*

DUNCAN — Perhaps a' shoulda told him then.

ALEX — What?

DUNCAN — That I'm clearin' all me old stock aht an' startin' wi' armour plate.

ALEX — Oh, are ya?

DUNCAN — The other men listen to him.

CONNIE — (*to* ROB) You'll brek yer jaw.

DUNCAN — They respect him.

ALEX — Don't they respect you?

DUNCAN — I didn't ask for this. A' said a' didn't want it.

ALEX — It wor already cooked for ya.

DUNCAN — I'm goin' 'ome.

DUNCAN *hands the plate to* ALEX.

ROB — I've done it.

ALEX — When shall a' see ya?

DUNCAN — A' feel sick.

DUNCAN *goes out.*

ALEX — Rob, can you eat this?

ROB — Yeh.

ALEX *gives the plate to* ROB *and goes.*

CONNIE — I enjoyed that.

ROB — They only had Mackesons. I prefer real beer.

CONNIE — No, all that talkin' a' mean.

ROB — Yer hardly said owt.

CONNIE — A' did, I argued on Michael's side.

ROB — Well, he's your brother. You stayin' 'ere?

CONNIE   With Alex, yeh. Left me husband. We fight.

ROB   What, is he a Blackshirt or summat?

CONNIE   He never stops thumpin' me long enough for me to ask.

ROB   Can't see the point in it me'sen: all that agitation.

CONNIE   It's ovver now.

ROB   A' wor gonna give them a piece a me mind; ya know, them two. Burrit went ahta me 'ead. I'd a bottle a beer in me 'and an' a' wor among friends, sort of.

CONNIE   Mek the best a things.

ROB   Yeh.

CONNIE   Bottles up.

ROB   Think I'll go east. Go as a missionary to Russia. Swim the Indian Ocean, plant spuds in China, sunbathe in the Arctic.

CONNIE   No ya won't.

ROB   A' know but I am goin' abroad, honest.

CONNIE   Is that the job?

ROB   Yeh. Is anybody else 'ere goin' abroad?

CONNIE   There's bully boys abroad: assassinations, bombins.

ROB   Look after me'sen. See to number one, see the world a bit.

CONNIE *holds her bottle up.*

CONNIE   Where to then?

ROB   Madrid, Rome, Berlin as well. Doin' up hotels; plasterin', brickeyin'.

CONNIE   Good money?

ROB   Rubbish.

CONNIE   Conditions?

ROB   Hundred hours a week.

CONNIE	An' no union.
ROB	Can't wait to get started.
CONNIE	Can a' come with ya?
	ROB *holds his bottle up.*
ROB	To you.
CONNIE	To you.
ROB	To the bugs in yer hair.
CONNIE	To the cardboard shoes ya wear. To the newspapers instead of underwear.
ROB	To the soup kitchen when the cupboard's bare.
CONNIE	To empty stomachs.
ROB	An' empty pockets.
CONNIE	To free speech.
ROB	To the future.
CONNIE	Cheers.

They chink bottles.

Scene Four

DOORMAN	(*off*) The doors'r open now. Keep the queue movin' please.
	MICHAEL *and* CONNIE *join the back of the queue.*
MICHAEL	Coz he's always sackin' me, see. So a' says to him, 'I'll save ya the trouble, I'll sack me'sen'. Shoulda seen his face. 'No need to be hasty Michael. Heat of the moment'.
CONNIE	He's frightened of ya.
MICHAEL	I've shook him up alright. No more ovvertime, slow workin', refusin' some work.

ALEX and DUNCAN join the back of the queue.

CONNIE He can't afford to lose ya. Wha'd'ya do now?

MICHAEL Naw, it's his move next.

CONNIE Can yer imagine it, Battersby's Military Armaments.

ALEX It's gonna rain on me hair-do.

MICHAEL Eh, we' leavin' a gap.

MICHAEL and CONNIE move down.

ALEX Connie. Connie, 'ere.

ALEX motions CONNIE over.

MICHAEL Speak a the devil.

ALEX Go 'n have a word with him.

DUNCAN Right.

As CONNIE moves along the bottom side of the queue, DUNCAN goes along the top side.

CONNIE Where's Duncan?

ALEX Come 'n tell me abaht yer trainin'. Hardly ever see ya.

DUNCAN Robson.

MICHAEL Battersby.

DUNCAN Humid, in't it?

ALEX They' talkin'.

DUNCAN Well, what's it to be? Strike, or no strike?

MICHAEL Strike?

DUNCAN Why can't ya treat it like it's just business?

MICHAEL I do.

DUNCAN No ya don't, yer too emotional ovver it.

MICHAEL I'm bloody not.

CONNIE Talkin'?

ALEX Discussin'.

CONNIE	Confrontin'. It's a family disease, bein' bolshy.
MICHAEL	Stop runnin' dahn apprenticeships an' brekkin' up blokes' duties, then mebbe we'll talk.
DUNCAN	Come again.
MICHAEL	Stop purrin' men on new jobs, or mekin' 'em do somebody else's.
CONNIE	I keep askin' questions.
ALEX	What?
CONNIE	Ahta the blue.
ALEX	What?
CONNIE	Nursin's run on very strict lines, yer s'posed to do as yer told.
DUNCAN	If you strike, how d'ya reckon I'm gonna keep yer all in work?
CONNIE	I interrupt matron an' ask her to explain things. She does.
ALEX	Wonder how they' gettin' on?
MICHAEL	A' wain't gonna call a strike.
DUNCAN	Can ya sign a piece a paper to that effect?
MICHAEL	Don't be such a big girl.
	DUNCAN *moves back down the line.*
CONNIE	A' say to the others, 'We the new breed. Don't get taken for granted, ask a question'.
DUNCAN	Waste a time, he won't listen.
	ALEX *goes along the line to* MICHAEL.
CONNIE	(*to* DUNCAN) He can be stubborn but there are ways a gettin' round him.
ALEX	What'll your wife say when she sees the size a yer wage packet this week?
MICHAEL	He's never bin the same since he went wi' thee.

CONNIE	First, ya tell him he's gorra wonderful brain.
DUNCAN	I ought to go back an' punch his nose.
ALEX	I'm surprised ya can afford to do this.
MICHAEL	I'll never forget when he brought yer on a tour a the works that time.
CONNIE	Next, you ask him for his advice. What he thinks you should do for the best.
MICHAEL	Course, a' wor watchin' him watchin' you, see. An' then I understood.
DUNCAN	I am gonna punch him, I've decided.

CONNIE *holds* DUNCAN's *coat-tails*.

MICHAEL	The big day soon, 'int it? Good job you come along. If he'd've chosen different we mighta still bin a goin' concern.
ALEX	Dun-can.

DUNCAN *runs along the line.*

CONNIE	An' if all else fails, tickle his feet.
DUNCAN	(*to* MICHAEL) What've ya said?
ALEX	He's bin rude to me.
DUNCAN	Wha'd he do?
ALEX	It's what he's said.
DUNCAN	Wha'd he say?
ALEX	I'd rather not repeat it.
DUNCAN	What've ya said?
MICHAEL	A' said ya wor a weaklin' an' didn't know yer own mind.
DUNCAN	Weak? I'm not weak. Wha'd'ya say I'm weak for?
ALEX	A' said he'd bin rude to me.

CONNIE *moves down the line.*

DUNCAN	Is that what tha thinks of me, after what I've done for ya?
MICHAEL	What's tha done?
DUNCAN	Tha's had a job sin' school, not many can say that.
MICHAEL	Oh, I'd a broken me back for yer dad.
DUNCAN	But not me.
MICHAEL	No.
DUNCAN	Right, yer sacked.
MICHAEL	What, again?
DUNCAN	There'll be no union, I'm gonna stop it.
ALEX	Yer ought to thank yer lucky stars yer in a job.
DUNCAN	A' just sacked him.
MICHAEL	Who do a' collect me cards off, you or her?
CONNIE	The air's gerrin' a bit thick. Blokes. Let's gerrit sorted before we gerrin there. Runnin' up 'n dahn the street. Michael.
MICHAEL	Connie.
CONNIE	We'll not gerrin at all if ya don't hurry. Go on, tell him abaht the morality of it, abaht his mekin' weapons an' that.
MICHAEL	It's nothin' to do wi' that.
CONNIE	Oh. Is it not?
MICHAEL	No. A' keep gerrin' misrepresented. A' just don't think he should tip everythin' upside dahn like he is.
CONNIE	Oh. So you'd say the same whatever it wor.
MICHAEL	Makes no difference to me what we mek. Length of the workin' week, each man to his own trade, underminin' the unions, that's worrit's abaht.
CONNIE	But don't ya believe that. . .?
DOORMAN	(*off*) Move dahn the line please. Nearly full now.

DUNCAN *and* ALEX *move towards the entrance.*

ALEX: Wha'd'ya tell him?

DUNCAN: Everythin'.

ALEX: He's dangerous.

DUNCAN: So am I.

DUNCAN *and* ALEX *go in.*

CONNIE: I've misunderstood what it wor abaht.

MICHAEL: I've no doubt yor heart's in the right place our kid.

CONNIE: But norrenough savvy.

DOORMAN: (*off*) There is room for one more person.

CONNIE: They gorrin front of us. Are ya sacked or not?

MICHAEL: I'm bloody confused. Morality? Never gi' it a thought.

CONNIE: No union.

MICHAEL: No union, no say.

DOORMAN: (*off*) One seat only.

MICHAEL: You go.

CONNIE: No.

MICHAEL: A' don't fancy it now.

CONNIE: You sure?

MICHAEL *gives her some money and waves her in.* CONNIE *goes.* MICHAEL *tosses the spare coin in the air.*

MICHAEL: Heads.

He catches the coin in one hand.

(*Without looking at it.*) Tails.

He turns his collar up against the rain. A clap of thunder. He looks up at the sky.

Scene Five

Dual action: 1. DUNCAN, ALEX *and* CONNIE *seated in a cinema;* 2. ROB *working on a building site.*

CONNIE Pathé news.

ROB *brings on a pair of stepladders and a pot of filler.*

DUNCAN What's the feature?

ALEX Things to Come, Raymond Massey. It's a great picture.

ROB *climbs the ladder.*

DUNCAN Seen it before?

ALEX Three times. Me 'n the girls.

(ROB *to someone below him*). What? War? (*Nelson-esque.*) I seen no wars. Me no see-o no guerr-o.

DUNCAN (*to* ALEX) That wor funny, Laurel 'n Hardy decoratin'.

CONNIE Let's listen to the news.

ROB Frank who? O? Frank O? Oh.

ALEX Did ya see Stan when he purriz foot in the paste bucket?

DUNCAN An' he turned round an' his ladder clouted Olly on the back of his head.

ALEX *and* DUNCAN *laugh.*

CONNIE Ssssh.

ROB Naw, he'll not come 'ere. They fight el battle in un field-o.

ALEX Is this the film?

CONNIE No.

ROB Let him come, won't bother me. Spain looks after its foreign nationals. We'll set the Uncivil Guard onto him. El Guardia Non-o Civilio.

ROB *points the wall.*

DUNCAN	Did ya see Olly's face when Stan pasted him to the wall?

ALEX *and* DUNCAN *continue laughing.* ROB *spins round, dropping his trowel.*

ROB (*looking into the distance*) Bloody 'ell, it's Frank O.

CONNIE	It's broken dahn.
ALEX	Can y'hear the rain on the roof?
DUNCAN	Yah. Sack the projectionist.

ALEX *and* DUNCAN *boo and hiss.* ROB's *ladder rocks.*

ROB	Wha'd'ya think you're doin'?

DUNCAN *and* ALEX *ad lib complaints.*

I'm doin' me job. El empleo. Am a' what? Tha' tell me whose side tha's on, then I'll know what to say for the best. Whose side am I on? I'm British.

DUNCAN *starts throwing sweets.*

Jesus wept. Machine-guns.

ALEX	Bring back the magic lantern.

ALEX *stamps her feet on the floor.*

CONNIE	Duncan. Who's Franco?
DUNCAN	One a the Marx brothers.

DUNCAN *joins in with the foot-stamping.*

ROB	Bombs. They' bombin' the outskirts.
DUNCAN	Here we go, it's comin' on.
ALEX	S'a bit loud.
CONNIE	What happened to the rest a the news?
ALEX	Oh look, it's started.
DUNCAN	It's the film. We've missed the beginnin'.

DUNCAN *and* ALEX *boo again.* ROB's *ladder rocks.*

ROB	You sods. Christ. I only came 'ere for a job. Gi' us a break. Have ya got nothin' better to do?
	DUNCAN *throws sweets.* ROB *ducks.* ALEX *and* DUNCAN *stamp their feet again.*
CONNIE	Where did they say that war was? Wor it Spain?
DUNCAN	We' tryin' to pick up the story.
ALEX	It's all abaht the future.
DUNCAN	An' this place is called Everytown.
ALEX	An' we're in nineteen fotty.
DUNCAN	An' there's a great war.
ALEX	Between everybody.
	DUNCAN *and* ALEX *watch the film.* CONNIE *stands.*
ROB	Speak English. No, a' don't speak Spanish. I am a visitor to this country.
CONNIE	(*remembering*) Madrid... Hotel Imperial... Aircraft bombardment.
ROB	A' know a few words. Bloody pigs. Chancos. Esta mas feo que un puerco.
CONNIE	Madrid. It wor, it wor Spain.
ROB	Bombs. Even closer.
CONNIE	(*shoving* DUNCAN *and* ALEX) Wain't it?
DUNCAN	What?
CONNIE	Rob.
ROB	Bastards. Bastards... What's the word for bleedin' bastards? (*Looks up*) Aeroplanes. (*With a pretend machine-gun, up to the sky*) Thackathackathackathackathackathacka-thackathackathackathackathackathacka...
DUNCAN	It's gone wrong again.
ALEX	No, we've jumped forwards. It's nineteen sixty-six an' they' still fightin'.

DUNCAN   S'a bit far-fetched this.

CONNIE   Robby. A' know he's there. Hi might be dead.

ROB   (*looking up*) Jesus. Looka them buggers. The noise they mek.

ALEX   (*to* CONNIE) Sit dahn. It's nineteen seventy...

DUNCAN   An' they' still fightin'.

ROB   A' can see the bomb doors openin'. How come it teks so long?

DUNCAN   I'll never forget Olly's face when Stan pasted him to the wall.

ROB *is catapulted from the ladder.* DUNCAN *busks the Laurel and Hardy signature tune.*

Dum-ti-dum dum-ti-dum
Diddle-i-dum diddle-i-dum
Dum-ti-dum dum-ti-dum
Diddle-i-dum ti-dum
Dum-ti-dum...

ALEX   Duncan.

CONNIE *has gone.*

DUNCAN   It's a load a rubbish this. When'r the cartoons on?

ALEX   Connie?

DUNCAN   Connie?

ALEX   She's gone.

DUNCAN   Prob'ly dragged her away in a straightjacket.

ALEX *thumps* DUNCAN.

(*Stan Laurel voice*) I'm sorry Olly, I didn't mean to. I thought we weren't going to fight anymore. And you said you weren't going to hit me ever again...

ALEX   (*transfixed by the film*). Listen. This is it, this is the best bit.

DUNCAN   You've watched this thing four times?

Pawnbroker Hocks the Moon

ALEX *superimposes her own voice over the woman's speech.*

ALEX You're exciting, you come from a different world. A world of blue skies, mountains, vast oceans. If I could see that world. If I could go with you in your flying machine. Your wings over the world. You men don't understand what imaginations we women have. Sometimes... Oh sometimes, I wish I were a man. I wish I were a man. Great, in't it?

DUNCAN Shall a' gerrus a cup a tea?

Scene Six

Hallway. Then mannikin—no clothes. ALEX *walks through carrying clothing.*

ALEX (*to the mannikin*) Wha'd'ya reckon Tarzan, think you'll get along with her? She snores, an' she leaves her clothes all ovver, an' she talks to her'sen. Pardon? Well, a' mean, it isn't normal.

ALEX *goes out.* CONNIE *comes in carrying a box.*

CONNIE (*to the mannikin*) I'll dress yer up when she's gone. Wha'd'ya wanna be? Maud. That's yer mistress yer talkin' abaht. Alright, ex-mistress, but they' not half-price skirts from the cheap shop an' she doesn't answer to Lady Muck. I've tried it.

ALEX *passes* CONNIE *on her way in.*

Just another armful.

CONNIE *goes out.*

ALEX (*to the mannikin*) No use fallin' for her, she's married already, to the hospital. I'll write to yer, a' promise. Look after Connie. Don't let her tek in any stray fellas, she's gorra charitable streak in her.

CONNIE *returns.*

CONNIE Have ya gorrit?

ALEX	I'll go. You'll not humiliate him.
CONNIE	Who?
ALEX	Tarzan.

ALEX *goes*.

CONNIE	(*to the mannikin*) Who? You've not bin seein' some bloke on the sly. Now I've told you abaht them. Seriously, a' think it's gone to her 'ead, all the money an' the big house.

ALEX *returns with bits and pieces*.

Hey, why leave so early?

ALEX	Gerrin' wed.
CONNIE	Six weeks yet.
ALEX	Four weeks three days. Stay in the new house an' decorate it wimme mam.
CONNIE	Haven't seen much of each other.
ALEX	A' wor always goin' aht as you wor comin' in.
CONNIE	Or you comin' 'n me goin'.
ALEX	A lot's happened. Anyway, I'm pleased you've come through yer bad patch.
CONNIE	Don't go.
ALEX	A' wor just tekin' these aht.
CONNIE	No, a' mean, don't go at all. Stay. 'Ere. We could be real friends.
ALEX	Gerrin' wed. A' know what you'll say but one bad marriage don't mek an avalanche.
CONNIE	Little miss One Per Cent. If there wor only one marriage in a hundred that worked, you'd still want to go for it.
ALEX	Or one in a thousand, or one in a million.
CONNIE	Don't end up like I did.
ALEX	I've got him like that. (*Thumb*)

DUNCAN	(*shouted, off*) Alex.
ALEX	In 'ere love.
	DUNCAN *comes in.*
	(*To* CONNIE) Well, most a the time.
	MICHAEL *comes in, unnoticed.*
DUNCAN	I've let the van go, it wor full.
ALEX	We can tek the rest in the car.
CONNIE	(*to* ALEX) Shall ya give up yer job?
DUNCAN	Wouldn't you? I would if I wor her.
ALEX	Worrabaht me pin money?
DUNCAN	Pins? (*About the mannikin*) Worrabaht this monstrosity?
ALEX	Tarzan.
CONNIE	Maud.
DUNCAN	(*to* MICHAEL) What'r you doin' 'ere?
MICHAEL	Lunch break?
DUNCAN	It's half-past two.
MICHAEL	Oh, nearly time for high tea.
DUNCAN	You've bin drinkin'.
MICHAEL	It's only coloured water when ya get right dahn to it.
DUNCAN	(*to* ALEX) Can you mek any sense aht of him?
ALEX	S'bad news whatever it is.
MICHAEL	Took me a while to find ya. It's important see.
DUNCAN	Connie, would ya mind?
MICHAEL	No, a' want a witness. Course, you'll not've realised. I've got the push, for real this time.
CONNIE	Naw, he didn't mean it.
MICHAEL	Didn't he? I heard the tone in his voice. Can he deny it?

DUNCAN   A' don't have to say anythin', you're diggin' the hole.

MICHAEL   Yer not interested then.

DUNCAN   Gerrit said, whatever it is. I've got things to do.

MICHAEL   (*to* ALEX) Enjoy the film?

ALEX   What?

MICHAEL   Things to Come.

ALEX   A' don't recall.

MICHAEL   Short memory. Wanna know the shape a things to come at Battersby's? A' know tha's interested.

DUNCAN   You tell Alex, then Alex can tell me.

MICHAEL   I've told yer men their jobs'r at risk.

DUNCAN   Well if ya wain't sacked before, yer are now. You'd no right.

MICHAEL   You've no right to sack me.

ALEX   Jumpin' the gun a bit.

MICHAEL   The early bird.

DUNCAN   Ya know what ya can do Michael.

MICHAEL   I 'ave, that's why I'm 'ere. Downed tools an' come away from it.

DUNCAN   You'll not be workin' again then.

MICHAEL   Not until you see reason.

DUNCAN   That's it then.

DUNCAN *goes out.*

ALEX   Duncan.

MICHAEL   Worrabaht the rest on 'em?

ALEX   Pardon?

MICHAEL   Yer precious factory's empty 'n silent. They all walked aht.

ALEX	Duncan. Duncan. Yer for it now.
CONNIE	Michael.
MICHAEL	Don't thee get caught up in it pet, it's bad enough I 'ave to.
CONNIE	How can I avoid it?
	DUNCAN *runs back in*
	There's three strangers 'ere, havin' a war in my hallway.
ALEX	He's called 'em aht. You've gorra strike on yer 'ands.
	DUNCAN *throws a punch at* MICHAEL, *who bumps into the mannikin, which falls over.*
CONNIE	Ya can hold it right there. These'r my rooms now an' if ya don't stop it I'll call the bobbies. S'like a bloody feud.
MICHAEL	I've come to tell ya that yer men'r in dispute with ya.
DUNCAN	Worrabaht?
MICHAEL	Proposed job losses.
DUNCAN	That's a bloody lie.
MICHAEL	An' you'll have to talk to me if ya want 'em back.
CONNIE	This is my place.
DUNCAN	Where's mister Mooney?
MICHAEL	Drinkin' tea, starin' at four walls, wonder in' how he's gonner explain his production figures.
DUNCAN	Me dad never had anythin' like this.
MICHAEL	Yer dad wor a businessman.
ALEX	Michael.
DUNCAN	He never had the same pressures.
MICHAEL	He'll be turnin' in his box.
DUNCAN	He wor cremated.
MICHAEL	Then his ashes'll be stirrin', like we just poked his fire.

An' we'll say, 'Come back aht John Battersby, we're in sore need of ya. Yer son's taken leave of his senses'.

DUNCAN Tha can't tell me nowt abaht me father.

MICHAEL No, but he could tell me more'n enough abaht his son. That he wor high-spirited but that his heart wor in the right place.

ALEX That's enough a that, patronisin' sod.

CONNIE Why don't ya just hang fire wi' the new work?

DUNCAN No.

CONNIE For a while. (*To* MICHAEL) Tek the men back in.

MICHAEL No.

CONNIE Carry on wi' the old work an' have a meetin' to talk abaht what's goin' off.

MICHAEL Too late now.

DUNCAN Michael, there's no point in this, me dad would've had to do the same. I'm tellin ya, we can't survive any closures. Shall a' gerron me knees?

MICHAEL S'the only way you'll get to know how I feel.

ALEX Don't be pathetic Michael, yer men won't love ya for that.

CONNIE Can't ya go into summat else?

ALEX A' can't stand this ball-a-string-'n-sticky-paper way a gerrin' things done. (*To* CONNIE) An' this isn't a public meetin' where everythin's up for grabs. I'll be in the car.

ALEX leaves.

CONNIE If ya told this story to a child, it'd laugh till its stomach bust.

MICHAEL I don't think yer up to this. You've certainly not got the look of a successful moneyspinner to me.

DUNCAN Oh hell yes, a' can turn me back on it, a' can forget the

	problem exists, that's the easiest thing. But how d'ya tell yer grand-kids ya took the easy way aht?
MICHAEL	The easy thing for me wor to pick up me cards an' get another job. A' could have.
DUNCAN	So it's hard for us both. An' how will it be if we can't deal with the hard facts of life? How will a city like this move from one day to the next if it's afraid to gerrits hands dirty? An' if it complains a scuffed knees in its scramble ahta the gutter?
	A car's horn is sounded.
MICHAEL	A' think yer wanted.
DUNCAN	I'll go when I'm ready.
MICHAEL	Strong woman you've got there.
DUNCAN	There's a dozen ways a showin' others how strong you are, but they count for nothin' if ya fail to convince thi'sen.
CONNIE	What's strong, mekin' weapons or not mekin' weapons?
DUNCAN	I don't care what you think abaht it, it's none a your concern.
	CONNIE *starts to pick up parts of the mannikin.*
	Either that, or feelin' stupid when a' said owt. Feelin' useless whenever a' tried to help with anythin'.
	DUNCAN *tries to help* CONNIE *with the mannikin.*
	Leave it. I'll do it. Wish ya wor as eager to listen to what I've got to say as yer are to do battle on my carpet. Which is stronger, knockin' people ovver, or not knockin' people ovver? Robby's ended up like this. (*To* DUNCAN) Bomb blasted. No good thinkin' abaht it when the tears'r already shed. Oh yes, we do cry. You wouldn't know—neither of ya—coz we don't live in your universe, do we? That's why a' stand her 'ere, in the middle a the hallway, so she's the main attraction.
	MICHAEL *picks the head up.*

Don't apologise.

CONNIE *takes the head from* MICHAEL.

I'll purrit back, after you've gone.

DUNCAN A' used to think it'd be great to have one final fling—ya know, me, Alex, Robby—one more night of the ritual madness. Forget you've gotten older an' taken on responsibilities. Burrit wouldn't work, coz ya can't ever turn back the clock. It'd be very very borin', not to mention embarrassin'.

CONNIE This is my place now. Never had a place of me own before.

DUNCAN (*to* MICHAEL) A' don't know what's gonner happen.

MICHAEL Whatever.

DUNCAN *leaves*.

Aren't ya proud of me?

CONNIE Is yer wife proud of ya?

MICHAEL She don't know yet.

CONNIE A' didn't think she would.

MICHAEL Difficult, 'int it? Knowin' what to do for the best.

MICHAEL *goes*.

CONNIE (*to the head*) Have yer ever seen a gang a girls playin' rugby? No, but why not? Coz they're afraid a what we'd say abaht them, in the scrum. Reckon that's why they do it, to talk abaht us? No, neither do I. They've got better things to talk abaht. They ferret themselves in there an' it becomes a secret society. The pack, the sweaty pack. An' they discuss things, an' they decide things, an' then they take action. But only they know where the ball is, an' only they know when it's gonna come aht.

CONNIE *puts the head back on*.

They do knock yer abaht, don't they?

Scene Seven

ALEX *and* DUNCAN

ALEX An' don't talk abaht the war.

DUNCAN Where d'ya think he's bin, Bournemouth?

ALEX Talk abaht the boozer, keep it jokey.

CONNIE *comes on.*

CONNIE His bus is just pullin' in.

ALEX Come on then.

CONNIE No, let him walk to us. Don't mek a fuss abaht his injuries.

DUNCAN We' not to talk abaht the war either.

ALEX Just act natural.

ROB *walks on using a walking stick, one leg in plaster. He carries a small suitcase.*

ROB Got blown up.

DUNCAN Papers've bin full of it.

ROB Got carried on a stretcher, Madrid to Guadalajara. Thirty-five miles in four days.

DUNCAN Bloody Italians, bloody Germans, why don't they mind their own business?

ROB We wor bombed on the road. Savoia 81s—Italian crates—screamin' ahta the sun.

DUNCAN There's bin a pit disaster at Barnsley. Fifty-odd missin'.

ROB They say you've got to go through these things to understand 'em.

DUNCAN That's right.

ROB Well I've bin through it an' a' still don't understand.

CONNIE *embraces* ROB.

CONNIE Welcome home.

ALEX: Eh, Robby. Remember Leslie Turner, Crabtree that was? Well, she asked abaht ya.

DUNCAN: A' could really go for her.

ROB: Married wi' four kids, in't she?

ALEX: Yeh, burrit wor good of her, wain't it?

DUNCAN: Lovely crabapples on that Crabtree.

ALEX: I'll never forget that all-night dance we had. Her ankles come up like footballs.

ROB *shuffles about*.

CONNIE: D'ya wanna sit dahn?

ROB: No, I've bin sat for hours. Just need to keep shiftin' me weight ovver.

CONNIE: Oh...

CONNIE *takes a small bundle out of her pocket. She recites*.

Flour of England, fruit of Spain
Met together in a shower of rain
Put in a bag, tied round with a string
If you'll tell me this riddle
I'll give you a ring.

Recipe for plum puddin'. The only child's song a' can ever remember. Thought it'd be a token, for where you've bin.

ROB *take the bundle*.

ROB: This'd be a luxury ovver there, ya couldn't afford it. The Generalissimo wants high food prices, low wages, no strikes 'n no newspapers. That's not the way to treat folk.

DUNCAN: Worrabaht Stalin? Open yer mouth too much ovver there an' it's showtrial 'n execution. (*Thumb across the throat*) No messin'.

CONNIE: Duncan.

DUNCAN	It's alright, Robby's bin around, he's got eyes in his head. Prob'ly knows more'n we do.
ROB	A' used to think a' knew.
DUNCAN	'Eard abaht them Welsh miners? Barricaded themselves dahn't pit.
ROB	The two men that carried me, they went on strike.
DUNCAN	For more money?
ROB	They wor on starvation wages.
DUNCAN	Wanna see what them Welsh buggers'r tekin' 'ome. Scots'r aht now. Colonials. Course it's all Michael Robson's fault, he started it.
CONNIE	It's bin quite a shock for ya.
ROB	Aye. When a' first went aht there a' thought a' wor badly done to. But a' wor in easy street, a' wor wealthy compared to them. So a' come back a rich man. D'ya understand?
CONNIE	Yeh, a' do.
ROB	If you'd've seen what I've seen, Connie.
CONNIE	Yer to rest.
ROB	If you'd've seen the blood. A' never knew a body could hold that much.
CONNIE	Yer not to think abaht it.
ROB	Don't ask me to forgerrit.
CONNIE	For the moment. Till yer fit again.
ROB	They drag dead horses along the street to form barricades.
CONNIE	Robby.
ROB	They burn the bodies of people where they lay, to prevent the spread of diseases.
CONNIE	I'm up to me elbows in blood every day.
ROB	S'not funny pet.

CONNIE	Neither's cuttin' limbs off an' post-mortems an' still-born babies. I'm a nurse.
ROB	Yer a nurse?
ALEX	An' you'll be better soon. Come to cheer yer up, like old pals. Mem'ries never did anyone any harm. A little reminiscin'. Remember the trips to the coast? Blanket tossins, snowball fights, swimmin' in the dam, the parties.

DUNCAN *sings*.

DUNCAN	Drewitt 'n Battersby Drunk on a Saturday Sober on Sunday In court on Monday On Tuesday they jailed 'em On Wednesday they bailed 'em On Thursday 'n Friday they kept out of fights

DUNCAN *cajoles* ROB *to join in with the last line*.

ROB & DUNCAN	But wor back in the boozer on Saturday night.

CONNIE *picks up* ROB's *case*.

CONNIE	Race yer to the car.
DUNCAN	I'll start her up.

DUNCAN *goes*.

ALEX	I'm so pleased to see ya safe back. No more trips abroad.

ALEX *goes*.

ROB	How'r things wi' thee?
CONNIE	Don't ask me abaht me divorce.
ROB	Does it matter?
CONNIE	I'd rather be free—officially.
ROB	Free... People think they are but they' not.
CONNIE	Yeh, people get pushed into situations.

ROB	An' kid themselves it wor what they always wanted.
CONNIE	Wear yer heart on yer sleeve, don't ya?
ROB	An' me pot on me leg.
CONNIE	Penny in the piggy if anybody ever mentions the Battersbys-to-be...
ROB	Or gerrin' a divorce...
CONNIE	Or any other kinda bad news, ever again.
ROB	Are ya sure it'll be alright? For me to stay at your place.
CONNIE	Who else'd put up with ya?
	ROB *hesitates.*
	What's up now?
ROB	Don't wanna go wi' them.
CONNIE	Can ya mek the tram?
ROB	Last one there's a cripple.
CONNIE	Gi' us yer arm.
	CONNIE *helps* ROB *to the tram. They forget the case. Off, a double blast on the car horn.* DUNCAN *comes on, followed by* ALEX.
DUNCAN	They've buggered off. Ya put petrol in the car for 'em...
ALEX	He's gone off with her.
DUNCAN	Left his suitcase.
ALEX	I coulda baked him a cake, or summat. It wor you. You did it wrong.
DUNCAN	What?
ALEX	Yer only interested in yer factory.
DUNCAN	Worrabaht thee, wi' yer trips dahn Mem'ry Lane?
ALEX	A' wanted to mek things right between us all. A' don't like

bad feelins an' bearin' grudges. What wor that, abaht Michael?

DUNCAN Oh, that wor nothin', just playin'.

ALEX Yeh, playin'.

DUNCAN What?

ALEX I saw ya, lookin' at her legs.

DUNCAN (*laughing*) Bloody hell.

ALEX A' know you've bin back round there.

DUNCAN A' wor pickin' that stuff up for ya, that ya forgot. You asked me to do it.

ALEX Well.

DUNCAN Is this part a the game, gerrin' married? Cold feet, emotional crisis ovver old flames, then mekin' it all up just in time for the big day.

ALEX A' don't want there to be any misunderstandings.

DUNCAN I'm too busy wi' work to go chasin' abaht like that.

ALEX You've bin workin' too hard, that's for sure.

DUNCAN Mebbe. Don't want any 'iccups.

ALEX I've seen big changes in you since Michael walked aht.

DUNCAN It'll be right. We'll have it shipshape, or not at all. Won't we?

ALEX Yeh.

DUNCAN Right.

DUNCAN *dangles the car keys in front of* ALEX.

D'you wanna drive, or shall I?

CONNIE *comes back on. She picks up* ROB's *suitcase.*

ALEX Are ya not comin' with us?

CONNIE He doesn't want to.

ALEX Oh. Why not?

CONNIE	A' think he wor close to tears.
ALEX	Why?
CONNIE	(*to* ALEX) A' don't think you should've come.
ALEX	I wanted to come.
CONNIE	And you always get what you want.
ALEX	What?
CONNIE	You know how he feels abaht ya. It wor coz a you that he went.
ALEX	No.
DUNCAN	Rubbish.
CONNIE	He wor a bright, silly boy when he left. He's come back like a bent fork, an' a' don't mean his leg.
ALEX	You'll poison him against me. He won't come to the weddin'.
DUNCAN	Are you gonna come, Connie?
ALEX	Duncan.
DUNCAN	You'll be welcome at the reception.
CONNIE	I'll be on nights.
DUNCAN	Yeh, so will we.
	DUNCAN *goes.*
CONNIE	Ya made the wrong choice.
ALEX	Oh yer really revelling in it. Yer new-found freedom. You've made good yer escape, you've taken a long breather away from all the turmoil but now yer back, dolin' out yer solutions an' yer cure-alls, like a good nurse should.
CONNIE	I've been there. Watch aht for his rabbit punch.
ALEX	Oh no, you wain't married that many years to be readin' me the old wife's tale.
CONNIE	We were taught to look up to men. To blush an' to give in

to their whims. To be ready in time, to be fit for use, to become what they made of us.

ALEX Well, men have got their urges.

CONNIE It's not just yer virginity that's at stake. Have you never stood back and had a really hard look at him?

ALEX Got the charm of a bull elephant, hasn't he? I'll take him, warts an' all. Ya can't stop men's urges, wherever they come from. Right or wrong, good or bad, hot or cold. They're as overpowering as the sea. Ya can't live without the sea.

Scene Eight

MICHAEL *breaks in through a window. He goes to one part of the locker room and collects some tools into a bag. He finds some workclothes and an old cricket bat. He stands in the middle of the room practising cricket shots.*

DUNCAN (*off*) Michael? Michael. A' know yer dahn there Michael.

MICHAEL Shit.

DUNCAN Mister Mooney saw ya climb ovver the side gate an' he sent for me.

MICHAEL (*shouts*) I've come to work. Ya can't run a factory wi' the gates closed.

DUNCAN It's private property an' I decide who comes an' goes.

MICHAEL There's others 'ere besides me. We're barricadin' the doors an' blockin' the windows.

DUNCAN I've got me keys Michael, I'm comin' dahn.

MICHAEL I'm settin' fire to yer factory Battersby, everythin's gonna go up.

DUNCAN We' movin' to the new place next month.

MICHAEL We' gonna burn together Duncan. Come on in an' feel the heat, feel the furnace.

DUNCAN   I've got insurance Michael.
           The sound of a key turning in the lock.
           Go on then, I'll only get half as much if I've to sell it.
           The door opens.
           Yer an intruder Michael.
MICHAEL   Me, an intruder.
           DUNCAN *walks in.*
DUNCAN   Michael.
MICHAEL   The familiarity of the man.
DUNCAN   Yer not wanted 'ere any more.
MICHAEL   I've come for me gear.
DUNCAN   Tek it an' get aht.
MICHAEL   I've got every right to be 'ere.
DUNCAN   No yer haven't.
           MICHAEL *drops the bag on the floor.*
MICHAEL   Worrif a' decide to stay.
DUNCAN   Tha wor always contrary, just for the hell of it. Obedience is a dead word to you. If a' told ya to stay you'd go. So stay, rot in the place.
MICHAEL   A' know every corner a this shop, a' know every smell an' every sound of it. In't that worth talkin' abaht, that kinda loyalty?
DUNCAN   Loyalty?
MICHAEL   Loyalty.
DUNCAN   I've got twenty men stood ahtside.
MICHAEL   Twenty men?
DUNCAN   They're not interest in your problems.
MICHAEL   Well tell 'em to buggeroff.
DUNCAN   All they wanna do is work.

MICHAEL Wha-?
DUNCAN They just wanna get in 'ere an' do the job.
MICHAEL Ahtsiders?
DUNCAN Twenty men formin' an orderly queue ahtside the front entrance.
MICHAEL Bastard.
DUNCAN All your men've bin sacked 'n sent packin'.
MICHAEL A' could kill thee for that.
DUNCAN Your power is gone. Yer dead wood, move ovver an' let someone younger in.
MICHAEL I'm only twenty-five.
DUNCAN Ah, yer an old hand at this game though.
MICHAEL Not old enough obviously, or I'd a spotted this.
DUNCAN You've gone mushy in the 'ead Michael, ya used to be a great thinker.
MICHAEL Ahtsiders? How can they know worrit feels like to've worked in this place all yer adult life? All me life, a' don't even remember havin' a childhood.
DUNCAN How d'ya think I feel? This is everythin' to me. I'm nothin' withaht it an' you're tryin' to wrench it from me.
MICHAEL How can they just walk in 'ere an' hope to understand worrit all means, worrit stands for?
DUNCAN Your feelins. These men've got more feelin' in their little fingers.
MICHAEL Desperate men'r unlikely heroes an' you're the livin' proof.
DUNCAN I've called the police, they'll be 'ere soon.
MICHAEL Police?
DUNCAN Trespass, fire threats...

MICHAEL *grabs hold of* DUNCAN.

If I can't instil order, 'ere, on me own patch, a' might as well give up the ghost. What kinda stability am a' gonner achieve if a' let whippersnappers like you rule the roost?

MICHAEL *raises his fist*.

Go on, thump me, burrit'll land yer in court. Yer livin' in the wrong decade. We need lions not camels. Your kind'r goin' dahn like ninepins. Unions? Socialists? Shall I add violence 'n thievin' to the list?

MICHAEL *lowers his arm*.

MICHAEL Them'r mine.

DUNCAN That's not very democratic Michael.

MICHAEL I own them.

DUNCAN If they're in this building they can't possibly belong to you.

MICHAEL You own them. Like yer new men. They're yours.

DUNCAN No. These men, they'll work for me, yes. Burra don't own them.

MICHAEL Yours, to set on or let go, as you choose.

DUNCAN My job is to run a firm. Listen, if I had my say everybody else'd have their say—everybody in the country—employers, customers, workers. Like a corporation. An' ya don't need no unions, nor no governments, to run a firm. When you've got one union for blokes that do it this way an' a different union for blokes that do it that way, what you've got is mish-mash. An' that's the food that governments 'n unions 'n socialists are weened on. An' don't they chew it ovver 'n ovver 'n ovver 'n ovver. . .

The sound of a police car's bell.

MICHAEL Did she put yer up to this? Mrs Battersby.

DUNCAN Why d'ya say that?

MICHAEL Coz marriage seems to've changed ya.

DUNCAN   I've not changed. An' there'll be no female influence in 'ere. Men thrive 'ere. Men only. Men that understand what team work is, an' what self help means. I'm a bigamist if anythin': married to the job as well. Team work an' self help, a modern marriage for the modern world. Those men ahtside understand tht, coz it's that kinda mixed bag that people want.

MICHAEL   Ya used to be able to find most of the men in my family in 'ere.

DUNCAN   Pity they coudn't a taught yer a little more respect for the place.

MICHAEL   Naw, I've always had that. But what I've learnt lately is that if ya don't do what the boss says, ya won't have no work at all.

DUNCAN   Modern science Michael, modern science. What were yer apprenticed at, before ya became a professional big mouth?

MICHAEL   Ya know damn well a' wor a file cutter.

DUNCAN   Oh yeh, yer great-grandad taught it ya. Now when wor the last time you saw a file cutter in this place of work?

POLICEMAN   (*off*). Mester Battersby.

DUNCAN   Well? What shall it be Michael? What shall it be?

MICHAEL *reaches for the bag.* DUNCAN *thumps* MICHAEL *in the stomach and knees him in the face.* MICHAEL *lies unconscious.* DUNCAN *picks up the bag and stands, waiting.*

POLICEMAN   (*off*). Mester Battersby.

Scene Nine

Hallway. Piles of clothing, small items of funiture, waiting for collection. ROB *carries a pile of stuff out.* CONNIE *sits, eating an orange.* ROB *returns and picks up another pile.*

ROB	How come women stash away so much jumble.
CONNE	How'r they gonna get it to Spain?
ROB	If we don't find some willin' helpers, soon, it won't be goin' at all.
CONNIE	Strap me into a harness, I'll pull the bugger across.
ROB	If you'd pull in a few punters, please.
CONNIE	Rag bone. Ra-ag bo-hone.
ROB	Connie.
CONNIE	They think yer collectin' for't bonfire.
	ALEX *comes in at the back.*
ROB	So yer not bothered.
CONNIE	Still thinkin' a Michael.
ROB	It wain't such a good idea me stayin' 'ere, wor it?
CONNIE	Yer never around. Yer so restless. S'posed to calm yerself dahn. It's lovely 'n quiet 'ere.
ROB	A' know but. . . Well. . . You've bin tekin' so much care of me. . .
CONNIE	Is that where I've got ya, on the end of a string?
ROB	I've gorra start livin' for meself again, sometime.
CONNIE	Yeh.
ROB	I'll do the collection.
CONNIE	An' have ya traipsin' the streets with yer gammy leg? You pull, I'll push.
ALEX	Nah then.
	ROB *drops the things he is holding.*
	Sorry. Didn't mean to frighten ya.
ROB	What' you doin' 'ere?
ALEX	Come to show ya me ring.
ROB	Ring?

ALEX	I'm married now.
ROB	Oh, yeh.
ALEX	Want some stuff for yer cart?
ROB	We'll call round.
ALEX	How's yer leg?
ROB	Oh, a' can go miles wimme leg.
ALEX	But not yer nerves.
ROB	Everythin' gets a bit much at times. A' jump at the least thing. Horses' hooves, thunder, sometimes a' can't even cross the road.
ALEX	When yer feelin' better, Duncan's gorra job for ya.
ROB	Don't wanna job.
ALEX	Still ahta work, aren't ya?
ROB	I'm doin' this.
ALEX	Don't pay nowt though.
ROB	Money's not everythin'.
ALEX	Changed your tune.
ROB	Could be worse off.
ALEX	Could ya?
CONNIE	He could be in the army. Mind you, just coz he broke his leg once, that won't get him ahta conscription.
ALEX	Come 'n work for Duncan an' you'll have no worries abaht that.
CONNIE	Yeh, munitions've always bin a job for life: gilt-edged.
ALEX	What's that supposed to mean?
CONNIE	Come on Rob.
ALEX	Hang on, I'd like a word with him. Private.
CONNIE	We've got work to do.
ALEX	How come you got so rude?

CONNIE	If you don't know, nobody does.
ALEX	A' don't know.
CONNIE	I don't know how ya keep yer face straight.
ALEX	Go on, pretend a' don't really know what's happenin'. Then ya can enjoy thi'sen, layin' it on double thick as ya reveal it all to me. Rob?
ROB	It's Michael, They've purrim in prison.
CONNIE	Ya didn't know.
ALEX	Why should a'? A' know that Michael broke into the factory, smashed the place up an' stole some equipment.
CONNIE	That what he told ya?
ALEX	That's the truth.
CONNIE	I'll not see Robby workin' in munitions. Weapons break people's legs.
ALEX	You'd like to blame Duncan for everything.
CONNIE	Nowt as queer as blokes. What they'll do, what they gerrup to, nobody's business. An' if the boss's wife wants an even newer house, no doubt there'll be ways 'n means a mekin' up the mortgage.
ALEX	People live in houses, it's an old custom.
ROB	Some don't. Some live like that, on a cart full a bits 'n bobs, their lives on two wheels.
ALEX	A' said I'd gi' ya summat.
ROB	That'd be yer house, yer sleepin' quarters, all yer belongin's.
ALEX	Ya can't expect me to carry the world on me shoulders.
ROB	That'd be the place where you ate, yer shelter from enemies, yer bed.
ALEX	So we bomb the bombers, we hit the buggers that broke your leg. Will that please ya?
CONNIE	No. It'll only bring pleasure to them that get new houses aht of it.

ALEX: Everybody 'n his dog mek weapons.

CONNIE: Well it's wrong.

ALEX: Men fight. So what? I used to find it flattering when they fought ovver me.

ROB *goes out*.

A good marriage, that's all I ever wanted. That's what a' come to tell ya: me marriage, it's great; a' love it, it's really fine.

CONNIE: He'd never have got where he is without you.

ALEX: Thank you.

CONNIE: You'll make a fine pair. He'll do the paradin' 'n the prancin' an' you'll pat him on the back an' applaud him for a good show. An' the more ya play up to him the more he'll do it, like a little boy showing off. You'll have us all in prison, or blown up.

ALEX: I'll see what I can do, as regards Michael. No promises.

CONNIE: Forgerrit. What's done's done. Yer a married woman now. An' there's nothing quite so ex as an ex-virgin.

ALEX: What?

CONNIE: Ya can't unbreak the law, not even for Michael.

ROB *comes back*.

ALEX: Ya can't say he wain't provoked, whatever he's done, or said.

ROB: Are we goin' or what?

ALEX: Be seein' ya.

ALEX *goes*.

ROB: Think she'll do anythin'?

CONNIE: Michael knew what the risks were.

ROB: I'm sorry. For bein' ungrateful.

CONNIE: Don't be daft.

ROB	Been a big help to me.
CONNIE	You help yerself best.
ROB	I'd go back there me. If a' wor fit, I'd go back there an' fight. People'r frightened.
CONNIE	What of?
ROB	Spain. That it'll lead to another war. Do you think it will?
CONNIE	No concern of mine. I don't have a say. An' I don't have the right to run anybody's life; only me own. Only me family's.

Scene Ten

Railway station, platform four. MICHAEL, *with baggage.* ROB, *who wears a red poppy.*

ANNOUNCER	(*off*) The next train to arrive at platform four will be the late-running five forty-five for London King's Cross. We apologise for the late arrival of this train, which is due to a points failure.
MICHAEL	An hour 'n half late.
ROB	They run on time in Europe.
MICHAEL	A few weeks ovverseas an' ya know it like a native. Wish tha wor comin' wimme.
ROB	Well.

CONNIE *rushes in. She wears a white poppy.*

CONNIE	Michael.
MICHAEL	I'm gerrin' this train. Then another, then the boat. More trains, through a city, ovver mountains... an' so on.
CONNIE	Don't go if it's just a favour for Robby. (*To* ROB) I'm sorry but it's got to be said.
MICHAEL	It's not.
CONNIE	Why then?

MICHAEL   A' need somethin' to get me goin' again.

CONNIE   Do the pools.

ROB   Wouldn't let him go just for me. Send him with a message half-way round the world?

MICHAEL   (*to* ROB) Gerrus a paper, will ya love? Please?

ROB *goes out.*

ANNOUNCER   (*off*) Will passengers standing on platform four please keep well away from the kerb. A through train is due in precisely two minutes.

MICHAEL   Voices ahta nowhere, tellin' ya where to go.

CONNIE   Yer not Joan of Arc, Michael.

MICHAEL   Somebody's gorra stick up for 'em.

CONNIE   Stick up for 'em? Like their Johnny's clipped our Billy round the earhole an' yer off to see his dad abaht it?

MICHAEL   Come on, Con, ya know it's more than that.

CONNIE   That's the trouble. You're gerrin' yerself ready to take on Ghengis Khan, Attila the Hun an' all-comers.

MICHAEL   It's gonner happen if we don't watch aht. An' if ya can see it comin' ya should go aht to meet it. Stop it in its tracks, not wait for it to creep up on ya.

CONNIE   Yer tekin' yer stand, aren't ya? A' can see it in yer shoulders: like slabs a granite.

MICHAEL   I hate havin' to say goodbye to folk... Sorry.

CONNIE   A' don't see how ya can justify it. It's ahtside a what ya know.

MICHAEL   A' know abaht fascists. A' can see that much. An' if the problem's there, starin' yer in the face, ya should go 'n try an' do summat.

CONNIE   You wouldn't know a Spaniard if ya fell ovver one.

MICHAEL   It's the principle.

CONNIE   Aye, your principles. Aren't ya just doin' it for thi'sen?

MICHAEL	Me'sen as well, yes. Aren't you?
CONNIE	Do what?
MICHAEL	Yer scared I'm gonna get me'sen killed an' yer thinkin' ow you're gonna feel after.
CONNIE	Ya gorrit wrong.
MICHAEL	'Ere's me train.
CONNIE	No. Stand back.

The through train rushes past.

That wor it. Ya can't go now.

MICHAEL	You'd a thought someone like you'd be only too eager to rush to the aid of the defenceless.
CONNIE	Why?
MICHAEL	Yer a nurse.
CONNIE	Coz nurses care.
MICHAEL	Coz nurses'r soft.

CONNIE *shakes her head.*

CONNIE	Hard a marbles. Clear-headed, everytime. That's why a' can think things through properly. This goin' to Spain. If ya wor goin' to rescue Robby a' could see it.
MICHAEL	But.
CONNIE	It's yer principles. That's what yer fightin' for.
MICHAEL	Yeh.
CONNIE	Not the country.
MICHAEL	What's the difference?
CONNIE	So ya high-tail it across there an' ya do disgustin' things to one lot coz they did disgustin' things to some other lot. An' that's supposed to make us all a bit more human?
MICHAEL	Workers'r shat on in every country, that's why I'm goin'. An' there should be no barriers should there, when it comes to basic rights.

CONNIE — It's none a your damn business. Yer mekin' their fight your fight but they' not forced to be the same thing. An' ya get there an' ya walk dahn the main street an' ya shout aht: 'I've come to save ya'. From what?

MICHAEL — From the murderin' bastards that's ruinin' their lives.

CONNIE — Who's gonna save them from you?

MICHAEL — Me? I'm gonna protect 'em.

CONNIE — Against invaders 'n ahtsiders.

MICHAEL — Yeh.

CONNIE — But you're an ahtsider, don't ya see?

MICHAEL *rebukes* CONNIE *with a slap across the face.*

MICHAEL — I've had to defend all my actions, to women, every day since a' can't remember when. A' shall look them poor buggers in the eye an' a' shall know we' brothers, under the skin.

CONNIE — Look in my eye. You 'n me, had a rough time of it. Makes ya wanna kick aht at everybody an' everythin'.

MICHAEL — If we hadn't've stopped the Bosche in France...

CONNIE — So this is your France. Coz ya couldn't go on the last one.

MICHAEL — Could be another Great War this one.

CONNIE — Prison's done this to ya.

MICHAEL — Prison wor easy. Do it wimme eyes closed.

ROB *comes on with a newspaper.*

You're leavin' me just as much. Proud of yer nursin', aren't ya? So why aren't ya comin' wimme? We' gonna need a lot of nurses.

CONNIE — Everybody always needs a lot of nurses.

MICHAEL — Be surprised how many've gone.

CONNIE — How many?

MICHAEL — Well... A' know there's some gone from Manchester.

CONNIE   Not heard of any goin' from 'ere.

MICHAEL   Must be coz they wear a red rose an' we wear a white 'un.

CONNIE   It's a poppy.

MICHAEL   Looks a bit pale compared to Robby's.

CONNIE   Where's yours?

MICHAEL   Is that how ya commemorate freedom fighters?

CONNIE   White is for peace.

MICHAEL   Yeh, that's what they died for, peace. Everybody lost somebody in the trenches. So we' got poppies, to remember the blood. An' that's why I'm goin'. Somethin' to do wi' bein' free. An' that's why Robby's wearin' red, coz he's seen the blood, gallons of it.

ROB   Still goin'?

MICHAEL   Yeh.

ROB   'Ere yer are then.

ROB hands MICHAEL a letter.

MICHAEL   There's no guarantee.

ANNOUNCER   (*off*) This is a platform alteration. Will passengers waiting for the London Express please make their way to platform one.

MICHAEL   Bloody' ellfire. Don't come ovver.

MICHAEL and ROB shake hands.

ROB   Keep thi' guard up.

MICHAEL   I'll write. Next week. Where wor it?

ROB   One.

CONNIE   We've always bin close.

MICHAEL   I'm not very natural wimme emotions.

CONNIE   An' I am.

MICHAEL   Too much sometimes.

CONNIE	Don't go.
MICHAEL	I'm not doin' this to upset ya.
CONNIE	Well yer certainly not doin' it for love.

ROB *holds out the paper.*

If ya don't run you'll miss it.

MICHAEL *goes.*

ROB	Forgorriz paper.
CONNIE	Self-centred bastard.
ROB	Not the way I see it.
CONNIE	There's others besides you, Robby. A' wor gonner ask him why his wife wain't 'ere. Didn't need to, a' could see it in his eyes.

Distant, the train departs from platform one.

He's gone.

ROB	I used to spend most of me time thinkin' abaht me'sen. But yer own problems seem unimportant when there's thousands a lives bein' wasted.
CONNIE	So why don't he wage war on the Don valley? On Battersby's Military Armaments: public enemy number one.
ROB	Fight Duncan?
CONNIE	Well Alex in't gonna stop him, is she?
ROB	Yeh, of course she will. She'll have him on toast for breakfast. Crusty strips of him—with marmalade—from now till the end a the century.
CONNIE	D'ya think so?
ANNOUNCER	(*off*). The train now standing at platform six is the seven twenty-five to Edale, stopping at Dore, Grindleford, Hathersage, Bamford and Hope.
ROB	(*reading the sports page*) Arsenal've beaten Leeds four-one. The Gunners: there'll be no stoppin' 'em now.

Scene Eleven

Night. ALEX *followed by* DUNCAN, *both dressed for bed.*

ALEX 'M cold.

DUNCAN Wanna go back inside? There's a big fire.

ALEX No.

DUNCAN Doctor said ya wor to get some fresh air.

ALEX What does he know?

DUNCAN He's a good man. Bin the family doctor for years.

ALEX Why don't he know what's wrong wimme?

DUNCAN It's nerves.

ALEX It's not nerves.

DUNCAN A lot a women'r like that till they've had their first baby.

ALEX Baby?

DUNCAN A' thought you'd a bin pregnant be now.

ALEX You hit me.

DUNCAN I slapped ya, to bring yer aht of a tantrum.

ALEX You hit me an' I've bin ill ever since.

DUNCAN When ya get pregnant you'll feel more relaxed abaht things. We'll have to try a lot harder than we have bin doin'.

ALEX Or you'll hit me again.

DUNCAN Alex.

ALEX If yer gonner hit me at least have the decency to admit yer hittin' me.

DUNCAN I only hit yer once.

ALEX Why couldn't yer have done somethin' for Michael?

DUNCAN *doesn't answer.*

Why couldn't yer have done somethin' for Michael? Offered him his job back.

DUNCAN You hear that Michael's gone aht to fight somewhere an' suddenly it's all my fault.

ALEX Who else wor gonner set him on wi' a prison record? Everybody's goin' to Spain. If you hadn't've decided on me, Robby'd never have gone. If you hadn't've had Michael purrin prison, he would never have gone. Do ya never think abaht the consequences?

DUNCAN He shouldn't a clocked me on the nose.

ALEX When a' wor sat in there, watchin' the fire, a' could see him.

DUNCAN Michael?

ALEX If ya stare in the flames for a long time ya can see pictures, faces. He wor laughin'. He wor laughin' at me.

DUNCAN Why should he laugh at thee?

ALEX To let me know that he knows.

DUNCAN Knows what?

ALEX Oh, I don't know, that it wor me that wor responsible.

DUNCAN Why do ya torment yerself? Yer not well. A' know it, a' know it, a' know it, a' can see yer not well.

ALEX A' know I'm not bloody well an' it's dahn to thee.

DUNCAN One gentle cuff across the cheek?

ALEX When we do things that damages other people.

DUNCAN Oh no, no, if we've got to have a scapegoat to answer for whatever's got to be answered for, let it be me. So it wor me, it wor me that did whatever it wor that wor done that wor so bad it's been givin' yer a bad 'ead. An' I'm sorry. An' a' promise it'll never happen again. What now? It doesn't mean a' don't need ya.

ALEX Ya need a damn sight more than me, Duncan.

DUNCAN Don't you ever listen? That wor the first time I've ever said anythin' like 'I love you', to anybody.

ALEX Is that what ya wor saying'?

DUNCAN A' thought a' wor.

ALEX A' want Robby to come 'n see me. He knows a' value his friendship.

DUNCAN Norra chance.

ALEX I wanna see Robby.

DUNCAN Yer my responsibility, your problems'r mine. We' married, we' man 'n wife.

ALEX He'll get his nerves back, won't he? He'll not end up mental, livin' on his own.

DUNCAN He's got more pals 'n cronies than leaves in autumn.

ALEX A' don't feel good abaht things. Somethin's not right. A' get nightmares, an' faces in the fire. They say it's like hell where Michael is. Wonder what hell's like? Where all the fires 'n flames were born. P'raps ya finally get to meet some of the people whose lives so nearly touched on yours but didn't properly. Eh, worrif ya turned aht to be the best a pals? An' that people ya thought wor enemies become friends an' the other way round. An' that really, everythin' wor opposite to the way it is 'ere. Bonny 'n blithe an' good 'n gay, instead a monstrous.

DUNCAN Which d'ya want me to be? D'ya want me to be different for ya? Stop bein' a monster an' chase away yer nightmares? Tek a good look round at what we've got. All this. A' got all this for you.

ALEX Don't say that, please.

DUNCAN Who else would a' get it for?

ALEX I'm not to be blamed anymore. You said you'd do the answering, not me. I'm a housewife, I'm not a bloody priest.

DUNCAN I don't know what yer fussing ovver. There's neither on us lack for anythin'. Us family 'n friends'r all alright. A' don't know anybody that's ahta work. All's well with our world. So I say we just go on, doin' exactly what we've been doin'. Coz if we go around givin' everythin' up coz we're in an emotional state, we'll be in one hell of a mess. Don't ya think? (*Tapping her on the chin with his fist—like a chum*). Somebody's gorra sit on the throne an' keep a watch ovver England.

ALEX What?

DUNCAN Didn't ya read it in the paper?

ALEX What?

DUNCAN Abdication.

Scene Twelve

ROB, CONNIE, DUNCAN, ALEX. *Crowd noises.*

ROB Think they' startin'?

The LORD MAYOR's *reading of the proclamation begins, over the tannoy.*

ALEX New beginnins. Wonder what they'll bring?

DUNCAN Money.

ALEX A bathroom.

ROB Time.

CONNIE Relax. Enter the new woman.

DUNCAN God save the King.

ALEX (*to* ROB) He hits me.

ROB Hit him back.

ALEX You hit him for me. Will ya? See to him for me.

DUNCAN You'll mebbe find this hard to believe Connie but once upon a time. . .

ALEX We wor all the best a pals.

ROB   Churchgoers together, sang in the choir.
ALEX   S'different nah.
CONNIE   S'different nah.

## WELCOME TO THE TIMES

Dave Sheasby

WELCOME TO THE TIMES was first broadcast by BBC Radio 4 as a Monday Play on 24 June 1985. The cast was as follows:

Fledge	MALCOLM HEBDEN
Celia / Nurse / Gospel Girl	DEBRA BURTON
Dawlish	NICK STRINGER
Joe	GRAHAM ROBERTS
Barmaid / Girl in Park / Porno Actress / Gospel Singer	CARRIE DAVIES
Slatterthwaite	BERT PARNABY
Kennedy / Taxi man / Gospel Singer	COLIN STARKEY
Mrs. S / Gospel Singer	ROSALIE WILLIAMS
Chocolate Worker / Woman on Bus	DAPHNE OXENFORD
Commissionaire / Tannoy Voice	RANDAL HERLEY
Hilton	PETER WOODTHORPE
Kramer / Porno Actor	BRIAN SOUTHWOOD
Baxter F.	SEAN BARRETT
Duggie	FINE-TIME FONTAYNE

Directed by ROBERT COOPER
Music by RAY ASHCROFT

FLEDGE The city first. Sullen, grey, widowed in the November rain, crisp as lace in May sunshine, empty as an echo on Sundays and at night sharp as a razor and sometimes dangerous. Cupped in hills this city and fed by tumbling rivers which race down from the purple fringe of moorland into its black heart. Stained by its past, made brittle this city, a civic pride dwells here. People say so. There's history on the streets and tradition. A modest but gritty northern-country identity. The city first and the people. People like me. Fledge. A local name. Two hundred years old they reckon, father's father, back to the early mills and workshops and forges, a long line of craftsmen down the years to this sudden vicious full stop. Out of work, jobless, redundant, scrapped. The last Fledge in a craft wrapped in its shroud and museumed up for the wet Sunday visitors. I left school at 14 for the forge. Like my dad before me. Word of mouth job then, never mind school exams or reports. 'Arthur's lad, when can you start,' and 'I hope you're a grafter like your old fella'. All that, a working lifetime ago. But now it's gone. Closed, shut down. The slow death of the old north and I was there and saw it all and will remember. The factories silent, the workshops empty and boarded. 'Vacant possess' boards hopeless in the rain; behind locked doors the machines rusting, the last works-outing notice yellowing on the damp wall. Toil, industry, labour. All the making days. Time for the veil to be drawn. Like the doctor said, the doctor with the green Porsche and the packed sullen surgery, 'Self pity gets you nowhere', so I washed his tranquillisers down the kitchen sink. It was while I was walking the city streets with my skills going rusty and the redundancy money dribbling away by the hour that I got the hint of a job. In the Crawford Arms, city centre pub jostled by solicitors clerks ordering their quiches and chillies. Some face from the past told me Dawlish was looking for someone. A chance conversation. A whisper, 'Don't tell him I told you, just say you've heard he's on the lookout for likely people, like yourself Fledge. Grafters. Dawlish likes grafters'. What had I got to lose? I'd heard of Dawlish. The name was on big lorries and new shops. It was in the papers and on quickfire TV adverts. The name was in the air. I rang the number from a callbox.

We have faded up a phonebox in a city-centre pedestrian precinct: the sound of a distant receiver as it is picked up.

CELIA (*distant*) Dawlish. Can I help you?

FLEDGE (*phonebox*) I've heard you've a vacancy. A job. I was wondering if it's been taken.

CELIA (*distant*) Just one moment please.

Click, silence.

FLEDGE (*narrates*) From the phonebox I watched 'Kamikazi Sam' turning over the contents of a litter-bin like the connoisseur he was. Kamikazi was a regular. People said he'd been a Spitfire pilot decorated by the king. A leather girl entwined a chain mail boy against the flat grey wall of a bank. To the lunchtime crowds, a man with a suitcase at his feet flashed cheap silver necklaces into the sunlight. On the phonebox wall someone had written 'No more wars please'.

Click.

CELIA (*distant*) Mr Dawlish says he'll see you now if you care to come round. What name is it?

Move from phonebox to exterior.

FLEDGE (*narrates*) A summer afternoon. I go by the weather. It sets the tone. Bright girls in bright gear were on parade. The last day of August. Straw hats were 'in' and the city centre was like a regatta day in some distant southern town.

A quieter back street—a few footsteps, perhaps a factory hooter.

FLEDGE (*narrates*) Dawlish's office was behind Dickinson's chocolate-button factory where women in turbans and green overalls made chocolate buttons for the world. A tiny square of silver plate on a steel door with the word *Dawlish*. A modest secretive label for an octopus empire.

Click of electronic intercom/lock on door.

CELIA (*intercom*) Who is it, please?

FLEDGE (*by door*) Me. Er. Fledge. I rang about the job.

CELIA (*intercom*) Come to the second floor, please.

Buzzer of lock. Door opens.

FLEDGE (*narrates*) I went inside.

Door shuts with an echoing crash.

FLEDGE (*narrates*) Two flights of cold hard stairs and then the office. Warm soft carpet, technicolour fish dozing in an ice-blue tank, chairs out of next year's design magazines, and at the mahogany slab desk, the girl. Wax-modelled, custom-made.

Dawlish's office.

DAWLISH You are?

FLEDGE Fledge. I rang. She said to come through.

DAWLISH Celia. My personal assistant. You like?

FLEDGE Er . . . very nice thanks.

DAWLISH Current favourite. Took some finding. We can learn from women you know. About loyalty, service, don't you think? My office. You like?

FLEDGE It's very nice Mr. Dawlish. No windows though, can't see out.

DAWLISH Windows are not company policy Fledge. Can't see in. Now what can I do for you?

FLEDGE	About the job.
DAWLISH	Job?
FLEDGE	Someone I met said you were looking for people.
DAWLISH	Someone you met?
FLEDGE	I don't know his name. Sorry. It was in a pub.
DAWLISH	I see.
FLEDGE	Said you had a vacancy.
DAWLISH	And you're on offer?
FLEDGE	That's right.
DAWLISH	Don't you want to know more?
FLEDGE	Well ...
DAWLISH	About what's expected ... the job description?
FLEDGE	I'm keen, punctual, available. It will suit me.
DAWLISH	The usual desperation. I am after, as it happens, a sort of round-the-house-round-the-office-person. What I want near me is someone who can clean the cars, take personal messages to business colleagues, drive me to meetings, appointments. Someone who can be on time you understand. Someone who is available. Someone who can keep their eyes open and mouth tight shut. Someone who can generally be of service and ten pound note reliable.
FLEDGE	I'm out of work at the moment.
DAWLISH	Course you are. The bloody city is. How old are you, Fledge?
FLEDGE	Fifty.
DAWLISH	That little hesitation ... fifty-two?
FLEDGE	If you say so, Mr Dawlish.
DAWLISH	Not a good start, Fledge. You'll find me watchful.
FLEDGE	I need the job, Mr Dawlish.
DAWLISH	Fit, are you?

FLEDGE   I think so.

DAWLISH Local, are you?

FLEDGE   Very.

DAWLISH Meaning?

FLEDGE   This is my city, Mr Dawlish. I was born here. Raised here. Worked here. I've never been away except for the odd week in Scarborough or Brid.

DAWLISH A son of toil.

FLEDGE   Sort of.

DAWLISH Steel, don't tell me.

FLEDGE   Yes.

DAWLISH Pity about what's happened. Still, he had a difficult job.

FLEDGE   He?

DAWLISH Chicago man. A ruthless strain. An outsider. No sentimentality. So, you want to work for Dawlish?

FLEDGE   A job's a job.

DAWLISH Do you know what we do?

FLEDGE   Sort of.

DAWLISH Basically we deal. Enterprise is on our flag and it flies everywhere. Enterprise. Heard of it, Fledge?

FLEDGE   I think so.

DAWLISH Know what it means? I'll tell you. Taking opportunities. Making the world work for you. Fixing to stay ahead, on top. You understand that, do you? Buying. Selling. Going for the space between the profit. Heard of it, Fledge?

FLEDGE   Is there a job, Mr Dawlish?

DAWLISH Wait outside. Five minutes. Watch the fish. Perfectly brainless I always think, fish. Important to have around. The other half.

FLEDGE (*narrates*) I waited with Celia in the outer office. I knew about Dawlish all right. A streetwise, jack-the-knife-city-slicker, quick-as-a-lizard, blunt-as-a-spade. He was a come-up-the-hard-way-haven't-I-just-number-one-is-number-one-flash-by-night-graft-by-day-on-the-maker. But what he really did and how and what he was going to do next . . .

Air-conditioned office again.

DAWLISH Can you start tomorrow?

FLEDGE Sure. Thanks.

DAWLISH Don't you want to know my terms?

FLEDGE Terms?

DAWLISH The retainer? The bait?

FLEDGE I'll leave that to you, Mr Dawlish.

DAWLISH It'll be on the palm of course. We don't want to get involved with the state, do we? Such a fiddly, messy crowd.

I will see you tomorrow, Fledge. Not here. At the house. Celia will give you directions.

FLEDGE Thanks.

DAWLISH You'll like it. There are windows at the house. I like to keep an eye on the gardeners. And watch the horizon.

Fade up pedestrian underpass below a dual carriageway: a busker is heard.

FLEDGE (*narrates*) I walked back to the town centre. Employed again. Somewhere to go. The meaning of work. In the underpass which joins the gun shop to Mario's pizza parlour a white-faced youth in an army trench coat busked to the going home crowd. I thought I recognised the song from somewhere but I couldn't quite place it.

We hear the song: then fade to silence.

FLEDGE The Dawlish house. Behind tall trees. On a misty September morning it loomed up like a liner. In charge of operations, Evil Mick, a youth in dirty overalls who patrolled the grounds in watchful, circular tours. 'Mick' was spelt out on the fingers of each hand in green tattoo, entwined with snakes. His black balaclava helped to chill visitors. The dogs raved when he went near. I was put on the cars. They just had to be kept clean. And the cassette music changed daily. The boss liked 'fine sounds'. On the third day Evil Mick told me Dawlish wanted to see me. His office looked out over the long lawns. Across the wall behind him a glittering blown-up photograph of the Rovers smiling across the green turf. I was a fan once.

They are in Dawlish's lounge.

DAWLISH   The team. I'm a director. You like?

FLEDGE   Er... I don't go anymore. Used to.

DAWLISH   They've done well. Since Morisco came. Have you seen him? From the slums of Brazil. He knows how to survive. Scores goals. Works hard. Running, running all the time.

FLEDGE   I've read about him, sir.

DAWLISH   That 'sir'. It really throws me.

FLEDGE   Sorry?

DAWLISH   I keep thinking I can hear a laugh somewhere. Never mind. Evil Mick. You get on?

FLEDGE   Er...

DAWLISH   I got him from Ragley. The nuthouse. You know it of course. Where the city keeps its troubles. The psychopath ward. There was a sale on. They don't know what to do with them. Overcrowding. The health cuts... I'm joking. He's on one of these youth schemes. I've got lots. They're very cheap and very keen.

FLEDGE   He says he's got a gun.

DAWLISH   Does he now?

FLEDGE   He keeps it in a drawer in the garage, he says.

DAWLISH Don't worry. Now, Fledge. I want your advice.

FLEDGE Sir?

DAWLISH You're local, you said?

FLEDGE Yes.

DAWLISH I am too. You know that though?

FLEDGE Everyone knows that, Mr Dawlish.

DAWLISH Do they?

FLEDGE About how you started with a wheelbarrow and some bricks and made your way up to shops and property.

DAWLISH Flattering. A bit exaggerated but then we need our myths don't we? I was born in Cartwright Street. Can't get more local than that can you? East end, east end. So near the works, the furnaces kept the house warm. Number 16. It's gone of course. Flat down. Good job too. My old man was at Baker and Slackleys.

FLEDGE They were a good firm. They've had some redundancies though.

DAWLISH Good firm? Your priorities amuse me, Fledge. The old boy worked there all his life, stayed poor but loyal, got sick and died. In pain. Good firm?

FLEDGE I meant—

DAWLISH I know what you meant. I watched the poor old dog cough his guts into the fire on his way to judgement day with nothing to thank anybody for, least of all Baker and Slackleys. Life was a sour pond for dad. At his funeral, we had him burnt of course, I watched his coffin slide in the wall behind those sickly purple curtains with that creepy music. Have you ever been to the crematorium at Partridge Wood, Fledge?

FLEDGE Only once. When a mate died. It was an accident at work. An ingot turned sharply. They didn't get compensation. The family I mean.

DAWLISH Tough. I expect he wasn't wearing the regulation gear. I

	always think the crematorium would be a neat investment if it went private. And it will.
FLEDGE	You wanted my advice.
DAWLISH	Slatterthwaite.
FLEDGE	Pardon?
DAWLISH	Slatterthwaite. The big boss at the Town Hall. Our beloved leader. King of the city. You know him? Personally?
FLEDGE	I did once. How did you know?
DAWLISH	What have you got on him in your filing cabinet?
FLEDGE	My—
DAWLISH	It's why I hired you. The local map. You go back a long way. Tell me about him. That bloody name gets me. Slatterthwaite. (*Mock Yorks.*) It shatters the teeth. He must have lifted it from a book. It can't be real.
FLEDGE	I went to school with him. Same neighbourhood. His mother cleaned up with mine. Shops and offices.
DAWLISH	Really?
FLEDGE	Ackley Secondary. We were friends. We had the same sort of interests. Beliefs.
DAWLISH	You don't say. Politics?
FLEDGE	Eric was dead keen even at school. We all called him 'Comrade Slatski'. He had Lenin pictures inside his desk lid. We joined the communist party when we were seventeen. There were quite a few of us did that after the war.
DAWLISH	And what happened?
FLEDGE	What?
DAWLISH	To you and politics?
FLEDGE	Lost interest, I suppose.
DAWLISH	Slatterthwaite is taking more time about it unfortunately.

FLEDGE   You don't like him Mr Dawlish.

DAWLISH   On top of the pile with his everlasting mandate. Lenin, you said? Slatterthwaite's in his sealed train. Local apathy will keep him there for ever.

FLEDGE   He's worked hard though. All his life. To build up the city.

DAWLISH   Prisoners of their own folklore, Fledge. Things have changed, that's what they can't understand.

FLEDGE   They've got power though. The rates.

DAWLISH   Too high for too long. Business is flying away, squawking.

FLEDGE   Education—the schools and colleges.

DAWLISH   Falling down and cracking up. They're like a bad client—can't deliver the goods but won't change the workforce. Or the shopfloor conditions.

FLEDGE   There's houses.

DAWLISH   Not much. Not anymore. What there is, decays daily.

FLEDGE   And there's all the services. I mean the council's—

DAWLISH   Parks full of dog shit and vandals, roads with pot holes in, theatres nobody wants to go to . . . the list is endless. Half the time these services are on strike. This week the bins, last week the busmen, last month the Town Hall clerks. It's so shoddy. I offer services. Cheap. Efficient. Accommodation—I've flats and houses. Transport—I've a coach firm and taxis and we do it cheap. Public works—I've a fleet of dozers and diggers. What I can't abide about the council is their interference. It's the death of efficiency.

FLEDGE   I don't see—

DAWLISH   And don't say it's democracy. We know now people are too lazy for *that*. How would you like to renew your friendship?

FLEDGE   With Eric?

DAWLISH   That's right.

FLEDGE Why?

DAWLISH I like to know what's going on, that's why.

FLEDGE What do you want to know, Mr Dawlish?

DAWLISH Anything you can find out.

FLEDGE He won't tell me.

DAWLISH That big new scheme to flatten the east end and build a whole new landscaped complex. It's going to cost millions. You could find out about that for me.

FLEDGE The Santiago Project.

DAWLISH Sounds like a cocktail.

FLEDGE It's after Chile. The revolution. 1977.

DAWLISH 1976 but never mind.

FLEDGE The council's dead keen on world issues.

DAWLISH The red flag over the Town Hall.

FLEDGE Only once a year, Mr Dawlish.

DAWLISH Pathetic. The little village is not big enough for them. So. Santiago. Anything you can tell me. Before it's too late.

FLEDGE Too late?

DAWLISH To make a contribution. I'm a civic man too, Fledge. We all are.

FLEDGE I don't think he'll tell me. It's been a long time since we were in contact.

DAWLISH Come on, you never know. One old red to another. There's a bonus in it for you. I'm good on bonuses, Fledge, ask the evil one out there on the lawn. Better not. Take a few days off. Leave the cars. Nose around a bit. Enjoy yourself. Find out what really goes on in this city of yours. Take this.

He takes a few tenners from his back pocket.

To be going on with. Don't stare like that at it. I do everything in brown ones. It makes people feel worthwhile, cash does. Only time my old man smiled was when he was opening his wage packet.

FLEDGE Thanks Mr Dawlish.

DAWLISH Only you don't know me do you?

FLEDGE I—

DAWLISH You're on your own. That's very important. I'm not known. For the time being anyway. You understand me I think.

FLEDGE (*narrates*) It was true. I did know Eric Slatterthwaite. I didn't tell Dawlish just how well. I knew him when he was ten and swapping his sweet ration for comics. We did go to the same sec. mod. One of the first after the act. The teachers hated him. Markham, the English teacher called him a bloody little shop steward but that didn't work. When Eric found out what shop stewards were he became one as soon as he could. He was bright too but didn't show them that at Ackley Sec. Mod. in case they shoved him in the A-stream. He won the school mock election in 1948 with a landslide for Labour and stood up in assembly and shouted 'We are the masters now' when the head announced the result. He got caned for it. Afterwards he said 'There you are, you win the votes but they've still got the big sticks to beat you with'. Once we went to Brid. on a fishing trip, got pissed and finished up at the edge of the sea shouting at the gulls above the waves about the end of capitalism and the coming of the revolution. Comrade Slatski. He worshipped Nye Bevan. Kept lots of cuttings. He was always making up bits of poetry and slogans.

FLEDGE (*sings/chants*)

'We'll set up Jack's republic,
We'll walk free down Jack's lanes.
We'll take back our coal lads
We'll take back our trains.
We'll make the people healthy
We'll make the people wise,
An end to all the bosses
An end to all the lies'.

He believed it, too. We drifted apart in the fifties sometime. Eric stayed in politics, got a bit softer, went on the council, mellowed but still kept his faith. Kept going. I followed his life in the papers. He's an institution now, still in there, fighting his battles, back against the wall now. They talked about a knighthood at one point. Callaghan's time I think. Not now of course. Maybe he'll get an O.B.E. One day. As compensation. Maybe they all will. When it's all over. If I was to meet him for Dawlish I had to make it look casual. I had to meet him on his own patch, accidentally-on-purpose. Joe Brackenbury would point me in the right direction and I knew where to find him all right.

Fade up betting shop under Fledge.

Joe Brackenbury. Once a first hand melter. The cream of the workforce. He could look into a furnace and tell them when, before machines could do it. The bosses needed people like that then.

Betting shop activity.

FLEDGE   How's it going, Joe?

JOE   It's our Fledge. How are you then? Not working are you? Course you're not.

FLEDGE   Sort of.

JOE   Sort of. Found somewhere open, have you, but you're not saying. I don't blame you.

FLEDGE   Paying is it? This?

JOE   Not much. Not often.

FLEDGE   I thought you might be in here.

JOE   Tell you what I'm doing now. A little side line. For my beer money. Don't tell the social people will you? I've got one of these little hand grinding wheels. It fits in my mac pocket. I go up round the posh end door to door and see if any of the ladies want anything sharpening. Scissors, knives, shears you know. They're quite intrigued some of them. I take a pair of scissors round the corner and sharpen them up and then I go back and say they can try them on my hair if they want to. I bend down and they have snip of my locks. They love it. It's like when the gippos go round. They're a bit afraid see. I only have to kneel on the step, a bit of a snip and they pay up. Sometimes they give me fags. Bit of cake.

FLEDGE You used to be a first hand melter, Joe.

JOE I remember. It's in my scrap book. What do you fancy for this one?

FLEDGE Monkey Man.

JOE You reckon.

FLEDGE It should get the distance and it likes the soft ground.

JOE I've done the favourite.

FLEDGE There was something.

JOE If it's a stable tip I don't want to know.

FLEDGE Slatterthwaite.

JOE What race is that in?

FLEDGE You still see him.

JOE Sure. In here sometimes.

FLEDGE In here?

JOE Fair shovels it on. And he loses. I've watched him. But then we all lose. That's the whole idea. What about?

FLEDGE I'd just like to meet up that's all. Old times sake.

JOE Try the Porter Lodge. Try tonight if you're that keen. He'll most likely be there. Late on.

FLEDGE The Porter Lodge.

JOE He goes in there with the magic circle.

FLEDGE Who?

JOE The little band of brothers who run the show. Y'know, Lawson from the trades council, that big head trade union bully Brygate, and there's a woman in it now, big lass with a sneery face and glasses. Not that they talk to me. Or anyone else for that matter. Not that anyone talks to them either. Folk are too busy with their boozing or fruit machines or million quid bingo or the jackpot lottery or anything else that might mean a bit of cash and make life seem worth living. That's how they've done it, see. Distractions.

FLEDGE They?

JOE Look at us in here now. Wall to wall. Like cattle. Obedient. Mind you it's useful. When it's too cold to stay at home and have the gas on. We call it the central heating club.

VOICE ON TANNOY Result Lingfield.

JOE Hang about for this.

VOICE ON TANNOY First number 6 Monkey Man, second number 2 Browning, third number 7 Menelek.

JOE You should come more often. Relieve the pain.

FLEDGE You're supposed to enjoy it.

JOE See him over there. The blackie in the suit. He's got a Mercedes round the corner. A very nice man. He owns shops and factories all over the county. He gives me a cigar some days. He told me once how he came here from Pakiland wherever ten years' ago with a suitcase and two tenners. Ever such a nice bloke. Funny I never saw a black one till I was thirty-five and now they give me cigars. Times change don't they, Fledgey?

FLEDGE Here. Buy yourself a couple of pints.

JOE Ta very much. You really are working aren't you?

FLEDGE (*narrates*) It wasn't just the politics that I fell out with all those years ago. Kath happened to me too. Slatski used to say women were a gate on the path to power—best jump over them quick. But then he was useless with girls. Too much of the roundhead, sack-cloth and ashes. 'A bachelor at 50, our Eric', Kath once said. She was right. Even so the way he used to look at her sometimes. Long time ago now. My lovely Kath. That morning she turned to me and said she didn't feel right. Odd. Far away. Couldn't explain it. The doctors did though. Illness. You get caught up. The outside world seem suddenly pointless and irrelevant. All that matters is getting better, possible change, hopeful signs. In the end, nothing. A big blank space. Back to work. Routine.

Fade up traffic in city centre at night: we just hear the busker.

Later that night after seeing Joe I went into the city centre to the Porter Lodge and crossing the road by the post office, I saw the white-faced kid again, singing that song. I still couldn't place it . . .

The Porter Lodge was packed and I pushed through to the counter looking for Eric.

Pub sounds.

BARMAID I wouldn't let them live if I got hold of them. Did you read about it? This poor old woman crippled, in a wheelchair and they broke in, killed her dog, chucked the cat out of the window and beat her up. For two quid. I wouldn't let them live. I'd put them in a boat far out at sea and I'd torpedo it and I'd let people watch for a bit of fun. What's yours, lovey?

FLEDGE (*narrates*) Eric was there all right. Anonymous as ever in that long grey gaberdine mackintosh. That same stoney face, impassive, watchful, waiting to make his point.

FLEDGE Half of bitter please. Evening Comrade Slatski.

SLATTER- I . . . Fledgey. Bloody hell. Long time.
THWAITE

FLEDGE A bit older.

SLATTER- Be my mirror lad. How are you?
THWAITE

FLEDGE Not bad, not bad.

SLATTER-THWAITE	Cautious as ever. You don't cross my path these days.
FLEDGE	No... well, you're a busy man.
SLATTER-THWAITE	Funny thing. I was only thinking about you the other day. Remember Markie, English teacher at Ackley.
FLEDGE	I couldn't forget him.
SLATTER-THWAITE	He died last week. In a nursing home in Scarborough. There was a couple of lines about him in the 'Chron'. Bastard. He lived to a very great age of course. They always do. Corporals and teachers.
FLEDGE	I was at Cromptons.
SLATTER-THWAITE	And that's gone. 400 was it?
FLEDGE	Near enough.
SLATTER-THWAITE	We're fighting it every day.
FLEDGE	So I read. Not with much success.
SLATTER-THWAITE	Tory lies, don't believe it.
FLEDGE	Empty order books they told us.
SLATTER-THWAITE	Aye, some guy lifts the phone in London and your job goes to Wigan or Wembley or Korea or anywhere.
FLEDGE	Would you like a drink?
SLATTER-THWAITE	This'll do me. I've a meeting later. Mustn't be cloudy. What are you doing with your leisure then?
FLEDGE	Not much.
SLATTER-THWAITE	We could use you. There's a lot happening.
FLEDGE	I read about it. See the billboards. 'Getting things done, taking care. Your council'.
SLATTER-THWAITE	Still cynical, Fledgey. Going it alone. 'You can't be in politics...'

FLEDGE 'And not get your hands dirty'. You used to say. Remember the world peace conference. 1951 You were trying to get on council that year *and* leaving the party.

SLATTER-THWAITE We had delegations from Bulgaria, Rumania, Hungary, Russia, the lot ...

FLEDGE Picasso came.

SLATTER-THWAITE That's right, he did.

FLEDGE He drew a dove in the meeting and they auctioned it off. I remember he stood up, waving this bit of paper.

SLATTER-THWAITE Bloody Picasso. Only thing I can remember is he couldn't speak English and he wanted a haircut. Story goes he went to Tommy Whittle's place and didn't leave a tip. Tommy was very upset about that. Picasso not tipping him.

FLEDGE They got it stopped, though. The conference. Sent the delegates home.

SLATTER-THWAITE Cold war, kid; what's new. Lots of memories Fledge. Lots of history. Our history. Some people have a vested interest in wiping all that out.

FLEDGE They've not wiped you out.

SLATTER-THWAITE It's not easy but we're still in there. Fighting. The main thing is to get on and do it and tell people why at the same time.

FLEDGE Like the Santiago Project.

SLATTER-THWAITE What about it?

FLEDGE I've read about it. Sounds very grand.

SLATTER-THWAITE It's jobs. It's improving the landscape. It's necessary. Someone's got to do things which are necessary. We've still got the power and we still care. That's what they can't understand.

FLEDGE They?

SLATTER-THWAITE	I haven't time. I'll have to leave you I'm afraid. I'd like to talk more but I've got this meeting. Policy. It's important. Come in again. I'd like to talk.
	Fade down pub sounds.
FLEDGE	(*narrates*) Half an hour to closing time. On the city streets. Some shouting youths vault the road barrier as two policemen with a dog watch from a doorway. Across the road on a bench outside the cathedral, two men in rags shared the dregs of a cider bottle waving it at the moon. The shop windows glowed and the Town Hall sat closed and dark as a fist. A little scene in a northern city on a late summer late evening. 'Just because it's quiet, doesn't mean nothing's going on.' As my dad used to say staring at the water. A fishing man. Watchful. Cautious. I fingered the money in my inside pocket, checking the notes Dawlish had given me. A generous man. And no deductions. Like he said I'd made contact. When I got home there was a note pushed under the door. 'Meet Mr Dawlish at his golf club at seven o'clock tomorrow morning'. There were directions. The note was typewritten on neat vellum paper that smelled of Celia. That night I dreamed of Kath. The usual dream—floating down the years . . .
	A golf course.
DAWLISH	It'll do. I'll settle for that.
FLEDGE	Nice shot Mr Dawlish.
DAWLISH	Looks as if my partner's lost. Peter Rickman. He's a headmaster. Rowley Wood. Know it Fledge? Comprehensive. It was nearly burnt down last week. Did you read about it? He's got trouble there. Some kids stole the geese in the rural studies department. Flogged them in the market. Clever boys. He wants me on his governing body. I'm only too pleased. If I can be of any use to the younger generation. Future customers after all. So how did you find municipal man after all these years?
FLEDGE	He was a bit busy.

DAWLISH He's so utterly blameless isn't he?

FLEDGE I don't think he's found his ball. Shall I help?

DAWLISH Slatterthwaite. He's proving very difficult ... Extensive research has failed to uncover any secret boozing; no excitement over ladies, gymslip or leather; no plain wrapper problem; no men's lavatory business or little boys; no cheating in exams; no cruelty to animals or women; no extravagance with consumer goods; he doesn't even stay up late at nights unless it's politics; he was a red once of course but who cares about that nowadays; he's really too good to be true isn't he?

FLEDGE He stole a packet of seeds once.

DAWLISH What?

FLEDGE When he was a kid. I was there. Nasturtiums. And he bets.

DAWLISH What?

FLEDGE He bets.

DAWLISH Are you sure?

FLEDGE Joe Brackenbury reckons so. He should know.

DAWLISH You've made my morning. I don't know how it got overlooked. I knew the Methodist ship leaked somewhere. Go and help the poor man find his ball will you? I'll see you on the green. You can help to appoint teachers when you're a governor ... did you know that, Fledge?

FLEDGE (*narrates*) Later at the Dawlish windowless H.Q. I waited with the fish for further instructions as Dawlish made telephone calls behind the dark door.

Fade up Dawlish's office.

DAWLISH I never thought. Ordinary money shortage. There we were looking for the dirty bits and all the time it was a question of petty cash. There's nothing on him at the banks. Frugal man always in a little bit of black. So it must be coming from somewhere else. Try these names, Fledge. Offer to pay for information and pass me the invoice.

Welcome to the Times

FLEDGE: Credit suppliers?

DAWLISH: Money lenders to you. The last life-line brigade. The pushers at the bottom of the pile. See what you can find out.

DAWLISH: Oh, and check the cassette in the white mercedes will you. It should be Mahler's second, the Resurrection. I can't trust Evil Mick. He's immune to music. It's the balaclava.

FLEDGE: (*narrates*) The pace was quickening. I began to feel interested. I had ticked off two names on the list as no success before I saw Kennedy. Briefcase, sheepskin coat, tiny sparrow eyes I was nervous. My old man always used to warn me against two things—the nobility and money lenders. He had some funny ideas, dad—for a forgehand that is.

KENNEDY: I'm a little pushed for time actually. Can we get to the business straight away? Do you have any current liabilities? I'm referring to dependents, hire-purchase payments, loans . . .

FLEDGE: Er, . . . It's not for me actually.

KENNEDY: Is this your own property? I couldn't help but notice the general dereliction—not for you?

FLEDGE: No.

KENNEDY: I'm sorry, I cannot act for a third party through an intermediary.

FLEDGE: I was really after something else.

KENNEDY: There must be a misunderstanding. We only lend cash on security. We don't provide goods, food, clothing. We leave all that to the Oxfam shop.

FLEDGE: I would like some information.

KENNEDY: We are a confidential service.

FLEDGE: I'm acting for someone else. He is prepared to pay, of course.

KENNEDY: A small fee is normally required.

FLEDGE   He has reason to check on the financial status of a colleague. He has to be careful in his dealings.

KENNEDY   Insolvency is a disease, Mr. er ...

FLEDGE   Fledge.

KENNEDY   Debt undermines. It's the worm in the wood. What exactly do you want to know?

FLEDGE   Just a yes or no on a name.

KENNEDY   Well now ...

FLEDGE   Like I said, we're prepared to pay.

KENNEDY   Would you care to write the name on here, that way this conversation never took place. You can't be too careful, can you? Pen.

The click of an expensive biro.

Fledge writes 'Eric Slatterthwaite'.

FLEDGE   There.

KENNEDY   Thank you. The short answer is yes. The name is known to us. If it helps you in any way I can say we are quite satisfied with the security provided. Family property.

FLEDGE   Thanks.

KENNEDY   A very big noise ...

FLEDGE   What?

KENNEDY   Our mutual friend.

FLEDGE   Oh. Yes. I suppose so.

KENNEDY   You wouldn't believe the people who come to us. One day someone will build a monument in honour of credit. On second thoughts it would only get daubed by glue-sniffing yobboes, wouldn't it? Good afternoon. I'll send our bill to you, shall I? Glad to have been of service.

FLEDGE   (*narrates*) Dawlish was very pleased when I told him. Celia was told to wheel in some good whisky. Afterwards we went for a ride on the motorway.

Interior of posh car on motorway—Elgar playing on hi-fi.

Dawlish liked to cruise in the outside lane flashing his lights at everything in the way. And the music, of course.

DAWLISH You like?

FLEDGE Very nice.

DAWLISH Elgar. The Du Pre version. So. He's in debt up to the elbows but he's pledged family property. Anything on that, Fledge?

FLEDGE I think it's his parents' house, Mr Dawlish.

DAWLISH Of course it is. Elderly couple. Out at Boughton. Right? Do they know you? The parents?

FLEDGE No. Eric was always mysterious about his mum and dad. He never took us near. I'm amazed to hear they're still alive. They must be getting on.

DAWLISH Fancy going to see them? See if there's anything you can turn over?

FLEDGE Can I ask you something, Mr Dawlish?

DAWLISH If you must.

FLEDGE What are you after exactly?

DAWLISH Some people find Elgar too ornate but I can't agree on that. It's business, Fledge. Pure and simple. As always. Dealing. I just want to play in the municipal park that's all. There's going to be so much to do. As the building crumbles someone's going to have to pick up the pieces and it'll be first come first served as indeed it should be. That's all. Lush yes, ornate no.

FLEDGE So why are we investigating him?

DAWLISH It's a market survey not an investigation, Fledge.

FLEDGE But—

DAWLISH Perfection's so dull isn't it, Fledge? When I was ten or so my dad took me to his works. A Saturday morning. I've never forgotten it. There was a tub of steel bars in a corner. I asked him what they were and he said they were scrap. They looked all right to me. Anyway he got hold of one and tapped it sharply on the wall. Crack. Just like that. It snapped in two. Like a pencil. A perfect white metal bar. Crack. Faulty. Flawed you see.

FLEDGE   You want to bang Slatterthwaite against a wall, Mr Dawlish?

DAWLISH   A metaphor, Fledge. It's so difficult here. The holy city I believe 'The Times' called it. Too many people in safe jobs playing fair. A chap can't make a living. Even the coppers are a bit straight. I only managed to buy off three last week. That's a joke...

FLEDGE   Oh... yeh... What do you want me to do now Mr Dawlish?

DAWLISH   Just go and see the old couple. Find out some more. I mean do they know Eric's put their house on the line? Do they care? It would make a lovely story if they didn't know. 'Town Hall supremo pushes ageing mum and dad onto streets'. The public detest heartlessness and cruelty don't they. And there's so much about.

FLEDGE   (*narrates*) All that time on the shop floor, that small world. Outside I never realised. Beyond the routine there were people like Dawlish who made it all work, set it all in motion. I took a bus out to Boughton. Someone had slashed most of the seats on the top deck. 'The stone-age is coming' was felt-tipped across a council notice offering cheap bus excursions. Still a bit of a village, half in fields, Boughton slept under the warm September afternoon. It wasn't difficult finding the house in a row of stone terraces, the gardens stuffed with green veg. and late summer flowers. The city hummed five miles away but here we were a hundred years out of time, how it all used to be. Dad used to say it was the big wars that changed it all. The big wars.

Fade up street in village—not very rural—some traffic—some birdsong.

Front door opened.

MRS SLATTERTHWAITE Yes.

FLEDGE Mrs Slatterthwaite?

MRS SLATTERTHWAITE If it's asphalting you're offering or the drains don't bother. The local radio warned us about you.

FLEDGE It is Mrs Slatterthwaite?

MRS SLATTERTHWAITE What if it is?

FLEDGE I—

MRS SLATTERTHWAITE You have to be careful at our age. People take advantage.

FLEDGE I'm from the Chronicle. The local paper.

MRS SLATTERTHWAITE I know what the Chronicle is. I've lived here 75 years.

MR SLATTERTHWAITE (*From inside*) Who is it?

MRS SLATTERTHWAITE A man from the newspaper.

FLEDGE I'm doing an article about Mr Slatterthwaite. The younger, that is.

MR SLATTERTHWAITE Who is it?

MRS SLATTERTHWAITE I should think so. Who'd want to do an article about the old one? Grumpy as a toad on fire. You should have to live with him. He's unsafe three parts of the week.

FLEDGE Can I come in?

MRS SLATTERTHWAITE I suppose so.

FLEDGE Thanks.

Fledge enters house—door closes—move to the lounge.

MRS SLATTERTHWAITE Meet my unspeakable lifelong companion.

MR SLATTER-   Who are you?
THWAITE

MRS SLATTER-   It's the man from the Chronicle. Mr . . . ?
THWAITE

FLEDGE   Johnson.

MR SLATTER-   A bit old for that game, aren't you?
THWAITE

MRS SLATTER-   Take no notice of father. He says he's in constant pain
THWAITE   with his legs but I have my doubts.

MR SLATTER-   Papermen. Usually spotty and useless in anoraks with
THWAITE   silly notepads.

FLEDGE   Er . . . I'm doing a series about local people's childhoods.

MR SLATTER-   What?
THWAITE

FLEDGE   Local V.I.P.s like Eric. What they were like as kids. I'm
                 just after some personal memories really. From ma and
                 pa.

MR SLATTER-   V.I.P. Is that why he's too busy to come round and see
THWAITE   us? We're still on the planet, you know.

MRS SLATTER-   The man doesn't want to hear all that.
THWAITE

MR SLATTER-   Mind you, we know he's still alive because we hear him
THWAITE   on the wireless. On the phone-ins. I'm going to ring him
                 up when he's next on and ask him to pop round. The local
                 radio never leave him alone. I think he's got a bed in that
                 studio.

MRS SLATTER-   The man doesn't want your views on the mass media
THWAITE   father.

MR SLATTER-   I call him the Red Shadow.
THWAITE

FLEDGE   Oh . . . really?

MRS SLATTER-   What would you like to know?
THWAITE

FLEDGE   Just a bit of background. About Eric as a lad.

MR SLATTER-   Comes round here for half an hour every plague year, if
THWAITE   he can remember where we live, that is, and then he's off
              to do battle with capitalism. Mr Fixit. You love him, don't
              you, at the newspaper? You don't look like a reporter
              ... You haven't got smooth white hands for a start.

MRS SLATTER- Would you like a cup of tea?
THWAITE

MR SLATTER-   Have you checked his credentials? He says he's from the
THWAITE   paper. Probably going to bang us on the head in a minute
              with a crow bar and take all our money. It happens every
              minute of the day, doesn't it? Bouncing pensioners—it's a
              national sport isn't it? It's either that or being run down
              by joggers. He does that next door. Jogs. He's from the
              Polytechnic. And his wife. They jog together. Like a pair
              of Shirleys. Time was these houses out here were just
              local folk. Not anymore. Pillocks like them now. They
              keep a goat, y'know, and she keeps trying to poison us
              with her home-made parsnip wine and they think our
              Eric's wonderful. Standing there in their steaming
              tracksuits saying 'right on for the republic' over the
              garden wall. I hide behind the compost heap.

MRS SLATTER- They're a very nice couple, actually. You know I can't
THWAITE   remember very much about Eric as a little boy. He was
              very quiet wasn't he?

MR SLATTER-   Pity he didn't keep it up. I blame Karl Marx, y'know.
THWAITE   Other kids had acne and football and trains. Not him. It
              was the Daily Worker with Eric. He never was a little
              boy. Coming round here every third moon in that silly
              Moscow hat with some scheme to help us in our old
              age.

FLEDGE   Scheme?

MRS SLATTER- I don't think the man wants to hear all our family
THWAITE   business, father.

MR SLATTER-   Doesn't he? What else is in the papers these days then?
THWAITE   That's all people do want to hear. Personal dirt and
              pain.

MRS SLATTER- Stamps. He had a stamp album. I think I've still, got it. A
THWAITE   whole set of Cape of Good Hopes.

MR SLATTER- Don't get the stamps out, for God's sake. At least when
THWAITE   he lived here we sometimes used to meet. Pass in the hall.
             Not now. Not that he isn't always on about us moving
             somewhere nicer, more manageable. She'll tell you.

MRS SLATTER- It is his house. Half of it anyway.
THWAITE

MR SLATTER- She doesn't know what's going on. She's eighty-three you
THWAITE   know.

MRS SLATTER- Just listen to the spring chicken. Eighty-one.
THWAITE

MR SLATTER- He even brought that civil servant round. Going on about
THWAITE   council houses.

MRS SLATTER- Father, now just shut up about—
THWAITE

MR SLATTER- Hilton. Rows of biros in his top pocket. Very shifty. And
THWAITE   there's our Eric hopping from one foot to another. It's not
             the first time he's been here either.

FLEDGE   Sorry. Who?

MR SLATTER- Hilton. Aren't you listening?
THWAITE

MRS SLATTER- Mr Hilton was just checking, that's all, and anyway you
THWAITE   have to wait your turn for a council house.

MR SLATTER- Council house—you'll have to get me in a wooden
THWAITE   overcoat before you get me in a council house.

MRS SLATTER- He gets rambly in the afternoons I'm afraid.
THWAITE

MR SLATTER- It's where my son gets it from.
THWAITE

MRS SLATTER- I think perhaps you'd better go, Mr er . . .
THWAITE

MR SLATTER- For a commie, he's very knowledgeable about house
THWAITE   prices, our Eric.

Welcome to the Times

MRS SLATTER-THWAITE
Could you ring us next time? Give us a bit of a warning? I might be able to talk to you better on my own.

MR SLATTER-THWAITE
I'll arrange to be deceased if it'll help. That's going to upset Eric the Red. When he has to take time off to see me put in the ground. He might have to miss a meeting. Forego the allowance.

MRS SLATTER-THWAITE
Shall I see you to the door?

FLEDGE
I can find my own way thanks.

MR SLATTER-THWAITE
You don't talk like a reporter. Meek as milk. They're a pushy crowd usually. Another thing. Tell your editor we know 'Spot the Ball's' fixed. Twenty years I've been doing it and never a penny ...

FLEDGE
(*narrates*) On the way back to the city, the bus picked up the 'first-outers' from Rowley Wood Comprehensive. They boarded like pirates and rocked it to panic point. In the city centre the evening paper placards signalled another rape in the Fulton Cliffe area. A 'beast' was at large again, the third this year. I decided to report to the boss. Celia was in tears quietly over her typewriter but she beckoned me to go through.

Dawlish's office is faded up—Dawlish is watching a pornographic video.

DAWLISH
Come in, Fledge. You like?

FLEDGE
Er ... interesting.

DAWLISH
Of course it is. Sex. One of the keys that helps us unlock the city. Not my taste you understand. I just like to check on any goods I sell. This stuff. It's booming. There's always another level to get down to. Novelty works here like everywhere else. A change is as good as a change.

FLEDGE
Distraction you mean, Mr Dawlish?

DAWLISH
So.

Enough flat flesh. (*Switches off*) To tell me?

FLEDGE	I went to see them. The Slatterthwaites.
DAWLISH	And ... anything useful?
FLEDGE	Well—the old man's not a fan of Eric's.
DAWLISH	Hints of trouble? The house?
FLEDGE	I'm not sure. Mrs Slatterthwaite was a bit cagey.
DAWLISH	Mothers. Defensive breed.
FLEDGE	There was one thing.
DAWLISH	Oh?
FLEDGE	Mrs S. got quite upset when the old man was going on about somebody called Hilton. Town Hall business. I could follow it up.
DAWLISH	Why don't you? You're enjoying yourself a bit now aren't you? Just a little. Better than humping hot wire.
FLEDGE	Ingot moulds. I was a forge worker, Mr Dawlish.
DAWLISH	Ingot moulds. then, if it's important to you.
FLEDGE	(*narrates*) It was important to Tommy Byron who died of burns on a routine strip that November morning but Dawlish wouldn't want to know about that. Anyway he was right in a way. I was enjoying it. The city was opening up for me. All those years of getting up, going to work, keeping my nose clean, the daily task, the graft—from where I was now, it was looking like a dream. I went to work because I went to work that's all. Celia was still in tears when I left the office.
	The sound of footsteps and voices outside factory.
FLEDGE	(*narrates*) Outside on the pavement the chocolate-button women thronged the turbanned road and there was talk of lay-offs and closures.
	We hear the voice of a woman as she passes:
WORKER	If I'm on the list our Ted says he's going to chuck himself in the river off Brunswick Bridge. I told him he might have to queue to get on the parapet. You've got to laugh ...

FLEDGE	(*narrates*) I started at the Town Hall. I remember; when I was a kid I remember going there with my mother and waiting while she tried to pluck up courage to go in. She had to apply there for a uniform grant and free school meals. You had to appear in person. They made it hard. She only got as far as the long grey steps and those big iron gates thrown open onto the dark hole of the entrance lobby and she never went no further. She hadn't got the nerve. So we trudged home and she scrounged a uniform and borrowed some dinner money for months before my dad found out. Those same iron gates and steps now. The echoey stone corridors; the atmosphere copied from a cathedral.
	Fade up exterior Town Hall—gospel singers heard.
FLEDGE	(*narrates*) On the forecourt a group of young people were singing about the coming of Jesus ...
	We hear a little of the song.
FLEDGE	(*narrates*) An old woman wrapped in old coats and wearing a black headscarf danced in front of them like an ancient squaw but the girl singer in the summer print dress just stared above her, glassy-eyed.
	Music stops.
GOSPEL GIRL	On a lovely morning like this I want to tell you some special news. I want to tell you, all you busy shoppers how to get served at the counter of the Lord.
	She continues to preach.
FLEDGE	(*narrates*) The crowds on the streets pushed past as the old woman danced and the commissionaire who shadowed the Town Hall doorway paced nervously tap tapping his white-gloved hands. It was worth a try.
	Interior of Town Hall.
COMMISSION-AIRE	Hilton? There are two or three I think. Do you mean Teddy Hilton? Housing? Charming bloke. Always time for a good morning. Worked here for years. Retired about a year ago. I've never seen him since. Walked out with his clock and whiskey bottle and flowers for the missus and

	he's never been back. Often the case with this place. People leave it behind with no trouble at all. Between you and me he liked a drink too. *And* his wife died shortly after retirement. *And* there was a bit of gossip about some building work. I'm going back now of course.
FLEDGE	Gossip?
COMMISSION-AIRE	Something to do with some firm getting some contracts for the council work. It all blew over but that upset him. Nobody ever proved anything of course. Just rumours. This place. Nobody really knows what anybody else is doing. Not like private concerns. That's a different story altogether. Mind you I'm not complaining. Stood here watching the world. I've got to watch the kids in the lavvies with this heroin lark but I'm lucky to be working, me. I was an engineer for thirty-five years. I was bloody *skilled* 'Chadburn and Slomans' since leaving school. Bust now of course.
FLEDGE	I'd like to meet Teddy Hilton. You don't happen to know where he lives do you?
COMMISSION-AIRE	I could find out. Trouble is it?
FLEDGE	Not really. I'd be . . . er grateful.
COMMISSION-AIRE	Oh. Yeah. Right then . . come back at lunchtime.
FLEDGE	(*narrates*) Two quid in the gloved palm was enough to find out where Hilton lived. Boston Green. I shared a seat on the bus with a woman whose winged glasses glinted in the sunlight and whose face was a landscape of anxiety.
	Fade up interior of bus.
WOMAN	Of course it's gone down, Boston Green. It used to be such a pleasant suburb. When Ken and I first lived there. Not much Green to it now, quite another colour now. The noise. The litter. When I remember how Ken and I used to play tennis on a Saturday afternoon and go for a quiet drink at The George on a summer evening. Perfectly safely. Without fear of molestation. Not anymore.

	It's all young people on motorbikes with language. At least we made damn sure we got Tamsin to a nice school. She's very happy at the High. It's all fee paying, of course, but Ken said we'd no real choice. We couldn't let her go to the Comprehensive. This is my stop. You want the next. Robert Road faces you when you get off.
FLEDGE	Thank you.
WOMAN	It used to be such a quiet leafy lane. Packed to the brim now of course. Only last week one of those families got terribly burned. They try to tell us it's arson, but it isn't you know, it's standards.

Cross to leafy student area—aeroplane overhead.

FLEDGE	(*narrates*) Robert Road. Big stone villas with clusters of bells announcing flats, students, lodgers, passers-through, front doors open to the sunshine, cats on warm steps, dirty milk bottles piled like ammunition. Hilton took a long time to answer his bell.

Front door opened—restrained by security chain.

HILTON	What is it?
FLEDGE	Mr Hilton?
HILTON	What if it is? Who are you?
FLEDGE	Can I have a word?
HILTON	What about? Is it a survey? You're the third this week.
FLEDGE	Sort of. I'm doing some research. I'm a student. About local government. The Town Hall people said to come and see you.
HILTON	What Town Hall people?
FLEDGE	You worked there I believe!
HILTON	Who are you?
FLEDGE	I thought we could have a chat. Over a drink. I've brought a bottle of sherry.

Hilton releases the security chains and opens door.

HILTON	Charlady's sunshine. Come in then. If you're going to bash me you'll bash me. I've nothing to pinch anyway.
	Close door—we are in hall
	Shall I take the bottle? British. That won't take us near fairyland will it? I thought you were from the social services. Interfering, poking about where they're not wanted. But the sherry's cleared you. That lot wouldn't bring sherrry.
	Sound of glasses.
HILTON	Here we go then. Shall I?
FLEDGE	Help yourself.
HILTON	Thanks. (*Drinks*) I've been left a year now you know. I don't think I'll be much help. And I've not been well. I've had these tests but they won't tell me what's going on. I'm under this Indian one. He shouts all the time. They say he's the top man but I don't trust him. Cheers!
	They drink.
FLEDGE	Cheers.
HILTON	The Town Hall. I could tell you a few stories. You wouldn't believe them though.
FLEDGE	I might.
HILTON	You wouldn't.
FLEDGE	Try me. Tell me what goes on behind the scenes.
HILTON	I . . . just a minute.
FLEDGE	What?
HILTON	Who are you?
FLEDGE	I'm a student. I told you.
HILTON	You're the dick aren't you?
FLEDGE	What?
HILTON	The law.
FLEDGE	I'm not.

HILTON	Legal then. Solicitor.
FLEDGE	I'm not, really.
HILTON	You're a bit old for a student.
FLEDGE	Funny. That's what Mrs Slatterthwaite said.
HILTON	Ah ...
FLEDGE	You know her? The old lady? Eric's mother? You know him of course. Working at the Town Hall.
HILTON	Everybody knows Slatterthwaite. Sieg heil. Can I? (*Drink*)
FLEDGE	Please. But you know him well don't you?
	Hilton pours some more sherry.
HILTON	What do you mean?
FLEDGE	Just that.
HILTON	I've been ill. Very ill. I have this nurse comes in . . . I don't have to talk to you.
FLEDGE	There was some trouble.
HILTON	You're a bloody newshound.
FLEDGE	No, I'm not.
HILTON	Talking to the Slatterthwaites.
FLEDGE	I've seen them, yes.
HILTON	Slatterthwaite's not sent you has he?
FLEDGE	Why should he?
HILTON	That little gang in the Town Hall. They can't hang on much longer.
FLEDGE	You don't approve.
HILTON	He thinks he owns the city. He's probably saving it for the Russians when their tanks come rolling up the High Street.
FLEDGE	I just want to ask you about—

HILTON That doctor. The way he looks at me. Fair progress he says. What's wrong with me? I'm ... dying aren't I? I'm bloody dying but...

FLEDGE Don't upset yourself. Have another. Come on ...

HILTON Living on your own. You don't know what it's like. The kids out there some nights. What do you want?

FLEDGE Just some background. Anything you can tell me about Slatterthwaite. I know a little ... council house?

HILTON What the hell does it matter now anyway? Who are you?

FLEDGE If it's any consolation it won't affect you.

HILTON Famous last words. He saved me. Slatterthwaite. I owed him my job. Pension. The lot. What does it matter now anyway. David's gone. South Africa. Doing very well. It can't hurt him now, can it? I dream about it you know, the Town Hall.

FLEDGE Who's David?

HILTON My nephew. I could never stand him. Margery hated him. And his slithery wife. I took a bloody risk for him. I can't imagine why I did it. Fat lot of good it did me. Few quid in the bank. Some booze money. We both saw that off. Margery was an expert. Holiday in Spain. It bloody rained every day. All for a little favour.

FLEDGE Favour?

HILTON I could go to prison for it you know.

FLEDGE What happened? With Slatterthwaite.

HILTON About five years ago David was trying to get this firm off the ground. Roofing specialists. A lifetime in that department and one day somebody suggests I earn a bit on the side. I couldn't believe it. Then I thought what could I lose? It was so easy. I had access you see. Access to the files and tenders. I was a regular. Part of the routine. I waited behind in the office and just took the file home with me and phoned the tenders through to David. I sat on the stairs with the phone and told him all the other bids.

FLEDGE What was the job?

HILTON Some school I think. The roof. It didn't even *feel* risky. So easy. All he had to do was bid lower. I only did it twice. After that they got lots of work. No harm was there? Only corruption. That holiday was a disaster. We were both pissed most of the time in the hotel.

FLEDGE Where does Slatterthwaite come in though?

HILTON He found out. The second time. I got into work early next morning to replace the files and he came into the office. He was like that. Still is. Always working, always poking his nose in. He rumbled me.

FLEDGE What did he do?

HILTON He let me off. Did me a favour. Turned a blind eye.

FLEDGE Just like that?

HILTON Very nice of him wasn't it? I had to plead, though. I had to beg. It had to be him who found out.

FLEDGE You don't feel grateful then?

HILTON You've no idea. The stupidity. The waste. It's not the little pen pushers like me, not the clerk and typists, they're all rushed off their feet. It's this new breed. Kids with Sociology degrees swanning about on cushy salaries in open-neck shirts and jeans and circus clown trousers getting things done for the people's republic. With their daft badges stuck all over them like a bad conscience. They're just driftwood that lot, spouting self righteous crap about any good cause under the sun—unemployment, peace, South Africa, abortions, homos. Talk about putting your mouth where your minorities are. Pathetic. Local government used to be about serving people with the basics. No fancies. No smart-alec stuff. But now, this lot have drifted in to take over the shop. Do you know what their favourite word is? Wanker. They all say it. Wanker this and wanker that. It's what they are but they can't see it. Pushing in the canteen queue and talking in loud voices about the latest campaign to save some coolies ten thousand miles away or open an advice centre to advise people and get themselves another job to keep themselves in petrol for the little Citroen. A lost tribe with a bit of power passing the time of day. It's tee-shirt slogan politics. Dirt cheap and comes out in the wash. It won't last. It can't . . . bloody hell. I'm sweating. Look at that. It's the sherry.

FLEDGE   Maybe you've had enough.

HILTON   Not enough. Nip out and get another bottle. Ha!

FLEDGE   Look I'd better go.

HILTON   So. What are you going to do with your information? Shop me? Shop Eric? I don't care. The nurse will be here soon. I pay you know. Private scheme. I had to. Hospital was no good. Ten months they said. And I was in pain. Staff shortages. Cuts. Ten months. So I went private. I had to. One of these schemes. You ought to join.

FLEDGE   You've never told anybody? About what was happening. The er . . . building thing.

HILTON   It's lethal information you've got there. At least if anything ever gets out that plaster saint at the Town Hall will go down with me. Cheers anyway. (*Bottle*)

FLEDGE   Why?

HILTON   Why what?

FLEDGE   I don't see Slatterthwaite's done anything wrong.

HILTON   Ah—I've not told you the whole story. Just before I retired, he came to see me in my office. He asked me a little favour. 'Trivial. Not at all important. Between ourselves etc. etc.'. . .

FLEDGE   What did he want?

HILTON   A bit of 'jiggery-how's-your-father' with the housing list. Ageing parents. You know how it is. Priority. Urgent case. They needed somewhere more manageable. Just a

	question of juggling the names round the list. He was very insistent. Shifty as a stoat. He was taking a risk. The names, you see. Slatterthwaite. I warned him about that.
FLEDGE	And did you? Er . . . juggle the list?
HILTON	Oh yes. But I'll tell you, I danced round the bloody office when he'd gone. If I was in his pocket, he was in mine. Imagine the relief. All those years with him on my back.
FLEDGE	So what's happened? Since I mean?
HILTON	I don't know I got ill shortly afterwards. I went for early retirement on grounds of ill health. I left it all behind.
FLEDGE	I'll be on my way then
HILTON	What are you going to do?
FLEDGE	You've no need to worry.
HILTON	I've quite enjoyed talking to you. Company. Come again, will you?
FLEDGE	I'll see myself out . . .
HILTON	Make it real Spanish next time eh?
FLEDGE	(*narrates*) I walked into Frimley Park, given to the city by steel king Arthur Douglas Laceman Frimley. On a bench someone had written in red felt tip 'Take now or stay the same'.
	The park.
GIRL	In need of anything?
FLEDGE	(*narrates*) Girl. Fifteen. Younger. Sullen mouth. Dark eyes. A boy shadowing her, shaven bomb-head and yellow smile . . .
GIRL	Electrical stuff? You know. Videos? Dead cheap. He can get them for you if you want. Can't you?
FLEDGE	(*narrates*) Boy nods. Yellow smile again. I shake my head. The girl moves closer.

GIRL	Anything else then ... you know ... anything ... cheap ... park-keeper doesn't bother. Let's me use his hut ... for a quid ... three for me ... that's all.
FLEDGE	(*narrates*) The sun is behind her and I squint up into her face. She puts her hand on her neck, tugs at her thin silver necklace, blood-red fingernails. The boy at her side grins again. I shake my head. I caught the bus back to town.
	Desolate sound of city.
	I walked up to Rainbow Park, the high-rise flats built in the fifties for a hopeful future by an architect who won a gold medal. A dream in the sky, they called it, but the housewives soon went crackers up there and the lifts broke and the rats moved back with their reputations intact. And the Russian and Japanese visitors stopped coming to gawp and the architect moved to private practice in London. On this warm September day up there on top of Rainbow Park the wind funnelled at me down the peeling concrete walkways and the slogan on a wall in white letters was 'Concrete city—abandon hope'. Back in the city centre Kamikaze Sam was moving from bin to bin, systematic and blank-eyed; the placards said 'Closures'.
	A car draws up.
	Electric window opened.
DAWLISH	Going our way?
FLEDGE	Mr Dawlish ...
DAWLISH	Get in.
	Door open/closed: interior car—they drive slowly through traffic.
DAWLISH	This is Kramer. Kramer, Fledge. Fledge is a colleague of mine. Very solid.
KRAMER	Afternoon to you.
DAWLISH	I'm just taking Kramer to the station. He's going back south. Can't get on with the provinces.

KRAMER Too many losers here. No style. It's really 'Fenchurch Street and Electric Company' territory. They talk about the north but I never quite believe it's going to be as bad as it is.

DAWLISH But you own some of it. Now.

KRAMER True. Acreage is acreage. Wherever you are, Fledge. Cash and acreage. They're the sun and moon on my planet. Mayfair and Park Lane. What are yours?

The car draws up and ticks over

DAWLISH Here we are then. I'll be in touch, Kramer. Nice to do business with you.

KRAMER Surely.

Car door opens.

Goodbye to you. Mr Fledge, go straight to jail. Do not pass 'Go'. Do not collect two hundred pounds.

FLEDGE Er . . . bye.

Door slams. Kramer goes.

DAWLISH Let's have some music. I've just done a deal. Rostropovitch I think.

Beethoven cassette inserted in hi-fi—it plays.

Kramer's big, you know. London based. They call him 'Mr Monopoly'. Funny man. He does everything in avocadoes.

FLEDGE Avocadoes?

DAWLISH Thousands to you and me. Don't ask me why avocadoes. The music. You like? Beethoven. To tell me?

FLEDGE You were on the right lines. Hilton worked in the housing department. Slatterthwaite and him sort of . . .

DAWLISH Tell.

FLEDGE According to Hilton, Slatterthwaite asked him to fix the housing waiting list. For his parents. About a year ago.

DAWLISH This Hilton. He's alive and well and ready to blab from on high?

FLEDGE It's not that easy. I mean, he's compromised. Slatterthwaite did him a favour. A big one. Covered up for him. Years ago.

DAWLISH Isn't it thrilling—life down civic street? Who would believe it? These sea-green bully boys with their pure white souls and stale slogans. It really isn't on, is it, not when the only thing in their favour is their goodness in the first place.

FLEDGE Hilton isn't much of a fan either, Mr Dawlish. I don't think he wants to get involved.

DAWLISH I want to meet Slatterthwaite now. You can fix that, can't you?

FLEDGE What shall I tell him?

DAWLISH Tell him I've a proposal to put to him. You go and see him on behalf of New Man Construction.

FLEDGE New Man?

DAWLISH He'll know the name.

FLEDGE He'll want to know what it's all about.

DAWLISH Say that it's private business.

FLEDGE He'll laugh me all the way to Bill's mothers. You don't know him.

DAWLISH But I do know him, Fledge. More and more. You must stress how important it is. Mention Kennedy. If that doesn't work, mention Hilton. The magic word.

FLEDGE I'm not sure he'll come Mr Dawlish.

DAWLISH He'll come. Your friend Slatterthwaite has done enough to hang himself from the Town Hall bell tower. People have gone down for a silver tea pot in his business. He knows that. And quite right too. Public money is at stake. It's their bloody job to be virtuous. It's on their hoardings, isn't it? Besides he's too fond of his own patch to take any risks.

FLEDGE	Where shall I tell him to meet you?
DAWLISH	My club. Thursday night. Seven o'clock. The happy hour. We do tequila sunrises at half price. You like?
FLEDGE	He doesn't drink.
DAWLISH	Never mind. Dawley's is the sort of place where spoil-sports come round a bit. Seven o'clock. You get out here don't you. And here's another flash for you. On the palm. Take care. It's not peppermint money that. (*Envelope.*)
FLEDGE	Thanks Mr Dawlish.
DAWLISH	Pleasure. Keep in touch.
	Fade car.
FLEDGE	(*narrates*) The High Street took me up. Still straw hats in the sunshine. Back to the Town Hall. A nod at the Commissionaire tap tapping his white-gloved hands and up the echoey stairs to the leader's office, past the notices promising 'services, solidarity and survival to those that cared enough to care'.
	Slatterthwaite's office in Town Hall.
SLATTER-THWAITE	I haven't got much time, Fledgey. I'm pretty booked up with meetings. Is it something urgent?
FLEDGE	Sort of.
SLATTER-THWAITE	I didn't think I'd see you again. After the other night. Thought I'd put you off.
FLEDGE	I just wanted to talk.
SLATTER-THWAITE	Not in any trouble are you?
FLEDGE	How do you mean?
SLATTER-THWAITE	Lots of blokes crack up after redundancy. I've seen it. What the government won't admit, won't face up to. The black side.
FLEDGE	It's not that.
SLATTER-THWAITE	You don't keep busy enough. You want to try one of our evening classes. Yoga. Bee-keeping. Social studies.

FLEDGE How do you do it, Slatski?

SLATTER- What?
THWAITE

FLEDGE Keep going. How do you hang onto your certainties?

SLATTER- I don't think about it, Fledgey. Politics. It's about getting
THWAITE power and keeping it and using it. It's not about getting the right 'line' every minute of the day. It's about hard work, meetings, committees.

FLEDGE What if you've got it wrong?

SLATTER- Tell me.
THWAITE

FLEDGE People don't trust you anymore. They've stopped believing.

SLATTER- People can be confused. Tricked. Our people easily.
THWAITE

FLEDGE Our people?

SLATTER- Our class if you want, but who cares what word you use?
THWAITE Fighting back. Hanging on to our objectives, the decencies, services, looking after those who can't look after themselves. It's so obvious what's wrong. I can't understand why there isn't more anger.

FLEDGE You really haven't changed have you? Since school.

SLATTER- Should I have? Remember outside the gates at Sharrock
THWAITE Engineering that time? After the wage cut. Waiting for Sir Arnold to come out in his silver 'Rolls'. I remember my face in the black shine of his limousine and him smiling in the shadows of the back seat. He was bloody laughing. And what's different now? There's still blokes outside factory gates shouting at bosses. Giros through the post doesn't mean anything's changed. I tell you it's still about the same old thing. It's nothing to do with Karl Marx and red flags and Russia. Not for me. That's just a side show for the media. The fellow-travellers who read the posh weeklies they lap all that up. And the Trotsky sixth-form debating society I keep treading on outside the Town Hall

with their damp pamphlets and buttonhole mouths. They miss the point because for them it's just words, headstuff. It's really about jobs and money and choice and power. Nothing's changed. But you haven't come to hear me make a speech though, have you?

FLEDGE Not really.

SLATTER- So. It's all yours. Make it snappy.
THWAITE

FLEDGE I've come to invite you to a meeting.

SLATTER- All a bit cloak and dagger, isn't it?
THWAITE

FLEDGE I can't give you names.

SLATTER- I don't do business with shadows, Fledgey.
THWAITE

FLEDGE Someone wants to meet you.

SLATTER- You're not making yourself very clear.
THWAITE

FLEDGE At Dawleys. On Thursday at 7 o'clock. Can you make that?

SLATTER- Dawleys?
THWAITE

FLEDGE It's a club.

SLATTER- Don't know any clubs. What's this about, Fledge?
THWAITE

FLEDGE It's important. To go I mean.

SLATTER- Who says?
THWAITE

FLEDGE I'm serious.

SLATTER- Then you're in dead trouble because I'm about to kick
THWAITE   you down the Town Hall steps, old son.

FLEDGE I don't think you quite know what you're up against.

SLATTER- All my life I've been 'up against'.
THWAITE

FLEDGE New Man Construction. I can tell you that. The name of the people.

SLATTER- Never heard of them.
THWAITE

FLEDGE They want to talk about a deal.

SLATTER- I don't do deals. I've officers to take care of all that.
THWAITE

FLEDGE They want to talk about Kennedy for a start.

SLATTER- Don't know any Kennedys.
THWAITE

FLEDGE And Hilton.

SLATTER- All these names.
THWAITE

FLEDGE I can tell you this, they know a lot about you.

SLATTER- I'm public property, kid. I've nothing to hide.
THWAITE

FLEDGE Haven't you?

SLATTER- What does that mean?
THWAITE

FLEDGE Only that . . . these people know one or two things which can't be too much good for you.

SLATTER- I've been investigated, have I? New Man did you say?
THWAITE

FLEDGE I think you should meet them.

SLATTER- It's a funny sort of job isn't it, Fledgey? For a steelworker.
THWAITE

FLEDGE Redundant steelworker.

SLATTER- Enjoying yourself, are you?
THWAITE

FLEDGE I was just told to deliver the message. Dawleys. Thursday night. Seven o'clock.

SLATTER- I know what this is. I've been around a long time.
THWAITE

'Mr. Twist'. He's always on the horizon in this game. And that's where he's staying. No deal. I didn't mean it about kicking you down the Town Hall steps. I'm too bloody old. And we're pacifists here, aren't we? Have you seen the posters on the stairs? You'll just have to get lost quietly.

FLEDGE (*narrates*) A nod to the Commissionaire who saluted smartly, remembering the two quid, and out into the late afternoon sun. I reported to Dawlish. I had to wait some time before Celia answered and when I got upstairs she was clearing away for the night.

Dawlish's outer office.

FLEDGE Late tonight.

CELIA Am I?

FLEDGE Is Mr Dawlish in?

CELIA He's with someone. I'm going now. You'd better wait. Have some coffee.

FLEDGE Right.

CELIA Goodbye then. And take care.

FLEDGE What?

Door opens.

CELIA Take care—that's all.

DAWLISH Fledge. Come in.

FLEDGE Evening, sir.

Door closed.

DAWLISH This is Mr Baxter-French, Fledge.

BAXTER-FRENCH (*South African accent*) Hello there.

DAWLISH We're just finishing. Drink John? Whiskey?

BAXTER-FRENCH Thanks.

DAWLISH Fledge?

FLEDGE Er ... yes please.

Drinks poured.

DAWLISH Mr Baxter-French and I were just talking about you.

FLEDGE Me sir?

BAXTER-FRENCH You and your tattooed colleague up at the house.

DAWLISH I don't think Fledge and he get on.

BAXTER-FRENCH You'll do fine, I'm sure.

DAWLISH Mr Baxter-French is referring to a few little deals we're about to embark on. Joint venture. Cheers.

FLEDGE Cheers.

BAXTER-FRENCH Santé.

DAWLISH We're hoping to get the distribution side going quite soon. We'll need extra staff, Fledge. If you know of anyone you could always give them a whisper, tell them I'm looking for someone, around-the-house ten-pound-note reliable ... lads at a loose end ...

FLEDGE What is it we'll have to do Mr Dawlish?

BAXTER-FRENCH Let's leave the details till later, shall we? It's a commodity. That's all you need to know. For the market place. Demand and supply. Goods and services. Exchange at the point of use. It's so logical isn't it, Fledge—economics? The science of God himself my tutor at Oxford called it. Mixing, as it does, the unexpected with the predictable in perfect proportions. You obtain the finest of rewards and the wickedest of punishments. Heaven and hell. I approve of that. We are the true radicals. Always have been. The open field of risk for profit. Don't you agree Fledge?

FLEDGE Suppose so.

BAXTER-FRENCH Who was it who said 'Gain rules OK'? Correction. I read

	it on a wall in a public lavatory in Jo'burg. This is excellent whiskey. I'll leave you with the samples. I suggest you think it over and get in touch soon.
DAWLISH	I'll do that.
BAXTER-FRENCH	Goodnight then.
DAWLISH	Goodnight, John. Mind how you go. Round here at this time. The streets.
BAXTER-FRENCH	Ah yes, the streets. The devil made your northern cities didn't he. Who said that or did I read it on a wall again? I'll be careful.
	Baxter-French goes.
DAWLISH	Very very neat. I admire that man.
FLEDGE	A bit strange. That black suit.
DAWLISH	He goes as far as the cabinet, Fledge. He goes as far as the oilfields and krugerrand gold. He's the honeypot, Fledge.
FLEDGE	What does he do exactly?
DAWLISH	He keeps up with the times mostly. Looks ahead. Sees what's coming. Actually, Baxter-French is very interested in personal security. It's going to be the next big thing here. To tell me?
FLEDGE	Sorry?
DAWLISH	Slatterthwaite?
FLEDGE	He chucked me out.
DAWLISH	Did he, now?
FLEDGE	I said he would.
DAWLISH	You mentioned Hilton.
FLEDGE	Yes and he was a bit thrown by that. I could tell. He played it big and don't care but he was worried I think. I told him about the meeting. He didn't give a definite answer.
DAWLISH	He'll come . . . take my word for it.

FLEDGE Celia seemed upset.

DAWLISH What?

FLEDGE Celia, tonight in the office.

DAWLISH Have some more whisky Fledge. He'll come.

The sound of a disco—voices loud but below level of music: fade so we hear it more distantly—we have moved to the entrance of the club.

FLEDGE (*narrates*) Dawleys. Early evening. Dark shadows, subdued lights and music to forget by. The doorman smiled and stood aside for me. I knew the face. Duggie Richards—'storeman' at Cromptons. Once.

DUGGIE Fledgey. How you keeping. You like the fancy dress? It's regulations.

FLEDGE How long have you been doing this, Duggie?

DUGGIE About two months. I was lucky. There were two hundred and forty others wanted it. I think the gaffer took pity on me. There was a girl with him at the interview. I think she fancied me.

FLEDGE Small world.

DUGGIE Bit out of your way this, isn't it?

FLEDGE I'm working.

DUGGIE Here?

FLEDGE All got to survive, Duggie. It suits you—the top hat.

DUGGIE You wouldn't believe it the money here. They drop me tenners on Saturdays. I never knew there was so much of it around in the town. Still, I mustn't gossip. There's two hundred and forty waiting for me to make a mistake. Do you know how I clinched it, the job? I lay on the floor at the interview and told the boss he could put his boot on my face . . . just give me the job . . .

Interior of disco.

FLEDGE (*narrates*) I sat at one of the corner tables, almost

	invisible and watched a near naked teenage girl dancing in her silver cage, her face expressionless, her little body jerking like a puppet.
DAWLISH	You like?
FLEDGE	Er . . .
DAWLISH	Maria-Helena. She came on one of those M.S.C. schemes. She was in the kitchen but with a body like that I reckon she's wasted on the slops don't you? I told her—upstairs, Tracey. That's her real name. Upstairs, lovey—more money, more fun, more clients. Where's our little tribune? It's five past seven.
FLEDGE	He might not come.
DAWLISH	He'll come. We'll wait.
FLEDGE	(*narrates*) At that moment Eric pushed into the half darkness. That long grey mack, that stoney face blinking at the strobe lights which raked him now and then and made him seem unreal and vulnerable. 'Up against it' again.
SLATTER-THWAITE	Fledge . . . evening.
FLEDGE	I thought you weren't coming for a minute.
SLATTER-THWAITE	Everything over-ran.
FLEDGE	This is . . .
SLATTER-THWAITE	New Man?
DAWLISH	Pleased you could come along.
SLATTER-THWAITE	Let's get on with it then.
DAWLISH	Care for a drink?
SLATTER-THWAITE	No thanks. Can we get straight on with the agenda?
DAWLISH	It's not a council meeting, Mr Slatterthwaite.

SLATTER-
THWAITE   More's the pity.

DAWLISH   I should sit down.

SLATTER-
THWAITE   No thanks. I'll stand.

DAWLISH   What do you think of Maria-Helena?

SLATTER-
THWAITE   What?

DAWLISH   The girl.

SLATTER-
THWAITE   Can you get to the point?

DAWLISH   O.K.—you want the blunt end. I'm Dawlish.

SLATTER-
THWAITE   Is that so?

DAWLISH   You might know my interests. Transport, accommodation, catering, leisure, property, insurance.

SLATTER-
THWAITE   Very nice. Where do I come in?

DAWLISH   The Santiago Project. I would like to be involved on the business side.

SLATTER-
THWAITE   I expect you would.

DAWLISH   It's a big development I believe.

SLATTER-
THWAITE   Millions. Look. I don't know why you want to see me but if it's business you do it through tenders. All above board. Personally I'd sooner have it all done by public works but it doesn't work like that anymore. We have to use people like you.

DAWLISH   We have tendered.

SLATTER-
THWAITE   If you're on the twist forget it. I've never taken so much as a chocolate button in this city, do you know that?

DAWLISH   Even so, I was hoping you could see your way to helping us out.

Welcome to the Times

SLATTER- Why should I do that?
THWAITE

DAWLISH Because of your reputation.

SLATTER- I'm happy with that, thanks.
THWAITE

DAWLISH You would be. You all are. What about Kennedy and Hilton?

SLATTER- Who?
THWAITE

DAWLISH All right. You owe a lot of money ... the gee-gees.

SLATTER- There's no law against that.
THWAITE

DAWLISH But we know you not only owe money you have also tried to raise some by getting your parents out of their house so that you can realise some cash.

SLATTER- My house ...
THWAITE

DAWLISH The point is you approached a housing official with a view to fixing a council house.

SLATTER- It's lies.
THWAITE

DAWLISH I think I can make it stick. People are prepared to testify.

SLATTER- Smearing, is it?
THWAITE

DAWLISH Come on, come on, you've been a bit silly, made a mistake. You're human. Don't keep waving your halo at me.

SLATTER- You can't just make accusations like that.
THWAITE

DAWLISH I'll leave that to the press. The public have to be told. That's what the press is there for. That's why you came, isn't it? Hilton?

SLATTER- I don't have to stand for this. I can snap you like a rotten
THWAITE twig.

DAWLISH Be sensible, Slatterthwaite. It's only a small favour. And I
can throw in an ex-gratia. Cash. Nobody has to know.
Think it over. Shall we say forty-eight hours?

SLATTER- I can fix nothing. It's all done by committees, votes,
THWAITE experts. You know that.

DAWLISH Forty-eight hours. At least let us know you're in. Or out.
O.K.?

SLATTER- I know you and your kind, Dawlish. I'd like you cast out
THWAITE of this city.

DAWLISH Pious hypocritical little shit. Standing there on your soap
box, self-righteous, holy-joe. Shall I tell you what you've
done for this city? Held it back. And for what? Your own
personal power. Man of the people. It's not about
democracy, it's about management, control, patronage,
influence. You're out of date; you're in the way.

SLATTER- I'm going to take some shifting, though.
THWAITE

DAWLISH I'll leave it with you. And if you're interested which I
know you are, there's a dog in race 7 out of trap 2 at
Bloxham Park on Friday night which cannot lose.

SLATTER- I don't do dogs—they're fixed.
THWAITE

DAWLISH Touching. Think about it councillor. You can do it if you
really want to. It's a small thing. I'm glad I've met you. I
wouldn't have believed it otherwise. You know that girl
really does have a flair for the cage, doesn't she?

Dawlish goes.

SLATTER- What are you staring at?
THWAITE

FLEDGE The girl.

SLATTER- Enjoying it are you? All this?
THWAITE

FLEDGE   You asked me that. It's a job, remember.

SLATTER- It's a mess. Bloody horses. I still go in I stand there. I've
THWAITE   got cash in my pocket. I'm sweating and I stand there ... paralysed. Don't ... don't.

FLEDGE   You can get treatment they tell me.

SLATTER- I don't need treatment. I just need a bloody winner or
THWAITE   two.

FLEDGE   Cool. Making jokes.

SLATTER- It's perfect, isn't it? Wouldn't it just suit this lot if I was to
THWAITE   fight back. Wouldn't it be a lovely way of removing me? Wouldn't it fit into their plans? And if I accept I'm in their pig sty. Very, very, clever.

FLEDGE   Look, have a drink.

SLATTER- Not with you, thanks.
THWAITE

FLEDGE   You really think you're special don't you? Above it all. You really believe in virtue. Yours and other peoples. The decencies ... you want to look around. The world's not like that any more. All my working life I followed the rules. The union. Fair play. What happens? Out. Finish. Forget it. Nobody really bothers. People do pick up phones in faraway towns. Like you said. You can't oppose it. You have to live with it. Take your chance where you can. People are on their own. It's survival. You get chucked out of work after a lifetime. You go home. You wait for something to turn up. You walk the streets. You wait for the giro. You take what you can when it comes. Decencies. You can't even live up to them yourself.

SLATTER- I'm going.
THWAITE

FLEDGE   Listen to me. Look around. Talk to the kids. Read their slogans. They don't know your history because no-one's ever told them. Talk to old people. Catch the fear. Confusion. Talk to the lads who went down with me when Cromptons closed. And all the others. They're on their own. Suspicions. Poverty stricken. Frightened.

	Lashing out. Taking where they can. They're not looking your way, Slatski, it's too late for that. You've lost them.
SLATTER-THWAITE	You're lost. You really are. You talk as if you'd invented despair on your own.
FLEDGE	All those years of striding round your little den, fixing this, arranging that. Putting out all the right hand-shakes, striking all the right poses. It's become a way of life. It's just a habit. You said—routine. You don't even follow your own rules ...
SLATTER-THWAITE	So you keep saying. I'm denying it.
FLEDGE	Hilton said it—it's a farce. Look behind you. There's no-one there following. It's like the song.
SLATTER-THWAITE	I don't know songs.
FLEDGE	Welcome to the times ...
SLATTER-THWAITE	I don't think I feel sorry for you any more, Fledge.
FLEDGE	You'll get in touch when you've decided.
SLATTER-THWAITE	Goodnight.

Cross to taxi interior.

| FLEDGE | (*narrates*) The girl in the cage twisted under the lights. I took a taxi home. I was frightened now, but there was something else. Exhilaration, excitement. It was like a dream—speeding, crazy, colourful. The taxi shot across the city. |
| TAXIMAN | I carry a baseball bat myself. Most of the lads have got something. Especially the coloureds. One I know's got a meat cleaver. Tell you what. I had a bloke in here the other night, very weird. All in the black and with this creepy voice. We got talking politics; they all want to talk politics and he leans over to me and he's getting out and he says how he agrees with me about things going rotten and |

he says 'that's it, isn't it ... the alsatian at the gate, the gun in the drawer and the fist in the face. The time has come'. He thought that was very funny. Gave me the creeps ...

Cross to a dog race meeting.

FLEDGE (*narrates*) Friday evening. Not a word from Slatterthwaite; Dawlish not available and Celia cold and unhelpful. I went to the dogs at Bloxham. After all I had a tip and spare cash. I decided on '50.

Suddenly the sound of a greyhound race.

FLEDGE (*narrates*) The dogs clanked out of the traps into the night glare and I shut my eyes. I needn't have worried; followed by Dawlish. The crowd roared the bitch home by two lengths. I turned and stared straight at Councillor Slatterthwaite.

SLATTER- Fixed was it?
THWAITE

FLEDGE Who cares? I thought you didn't do dogs.

SLATTER- I've come to see the messenger boy. Interesting firm, New
THWAITE Man. They've got a file on Dawlish at the Town Hall. This thick. Dawlish R.L. He's got a record. Lots of names. Many faces. Behind lots of doors, under lots of stones. And there's a girl in his office who talks a lot. Very upset about something. She really was most helpful.

FLEDGE What do I tell him, then?

SLATTER- No. Bad luck. Nice try. The jobs will be going elsewhere.
THWAITE Committees will meet. Votes will be taken.

FLEDGE He isn't going to like it.

SLATTER- Win and lose. Isn't that your game?
THWAITE

FLEDGE Risk.

SLATTER- You know the jargon by now.
THWAITE

FLEDGE He isn't going to be pleased.

SLATTER- Don't underestimate us, Fledge. Tell him that.
THWAITE

FLEDGE And Hilton?

SLATTER- I'm not going to stand by and watch it all smashed up.
THWAITE The last chance for a decent society. I believe it. I'm not going to give it up now.

FLEDGE Your power.

SLATTER- Yes. Power. It's bigger than me anyway. We're still the
THWAITE fabric of this place. We're not in shreds yet.

FLEDGE And Hilton?

SLATTER- No longer a problem. If he ever was.
THWAITE

FLEDGE He has some very interesting information.

SLATTER- Had. He's dead.
THWAITE

FLEDGE He's ... what?

SLATTER- Yesterday afternoon. He'd just been to the launderette.
THWAITE The home help found him. She said he told her about some kids he'd seen in there. He got worried and came home in a bit of a rush. There's been lots of trouble round there. Attacks. Anyway, he collapsed. She helped him to bed. He looked up at her, said 'Gin and tonic, Margery?' and died. I don't know who Margery was ...

FLEDGE ... He said the doctors wouldn't tell him.

SLATTER- I'm taking Dawlish on, Fledge. Oh, there's this (*Package*)
THWAITE I haven't counted it. It was on my doorstep last night when I got back from Hilton's. It feels to me like an 'ex-gratia'. Is that the word?

FLEDGE I don't know anything about this.

SLATTER- Take it back. I'm not bought that easily. Tell Dawlish no
THWAITE thank you to the cash and no thank you to New Man. And whilst you're about it tell him about us, Fledgey.

FLEDGE Us?

Welcome to the Times 151

SLATTER-
THWAITE
You and me. Barton Street. Where we were born, tell him about the night shifts; tell him everything, don't leave anything out, the past, the present, the paddling pool for kids or the mobile library for the pensioners and disabled; tell him everything Fledge, tell him about the jobless lads sucking on exhaust fumes or walking under trains, tell him what you've seen in the furnace flames; the blokes coughing up their guts in out-patients; the women queueing with the kids for a giro; scrabbling in the muck for a bit of coal; lining up for a loaf of bread, pinching from the meter to buy shoes, tell him, Fledgey, the history and what you know now. Tell him about shouting at the waves at Brid that time . . . Tell him about the lad who died in your arms in the forge screaming.

FLEDGE   How did you know about that?

SLATTER-
THWAITE
Because it's my *job* to know. Because anybody can know if they care to find out. See you around, Fledge. On the barricades. And soon maybe . . .

Fade out race meeting.

FLEDGE
(*narrates*) Slatterthwaite shoved the brown package into my hand and pushed his way through the crowds building up for the start of race eight. It felt like an avocado. Probably in tens. I collected my winnings on the last race and walked back to the city centre. A cool breeze had got up and there were flecks of rain in the night air. The weather was breaking. It was late to be on the streets—carrying what I was carrying . . . I would report to Dawlish in the morning. I needed to think it over first.

We have faded up on Fledge's home—the lounge.

FLEDGE *whistles gently (Welcome to the Times tune) and switches on light.*

DAWLISH   Evening, Fledge.
FLEDGE   I . . . you surprised me.
DAWLISH   Of course.
FLEDGE   How did you get in?

DAWLISH: Don't ask silly questions. Where have you been?

FLEDGE: Walking. I went to the dogs actually. Your tip. It went in. I hope you don't mind. I couldn't resist.

DAWLISH: Not at all. One of the perks of the job. To tell me?

FLEDGE: It's not good news, Mr Dawlish. I saw Slatterthwaite. He isn't going to ... deal. Tonight. He was at the dogs.

DAWLISH: At the dogs?

FLEDGE: He says your tender hasn't been accepted.

DAWLISH: He told you that, did he? Anything else?

FLEDGE: Er ... no. Just that you hadn't got it. He won't play.

DAWLISH: Be careful, Fledge. We are a big web. Flies get caught. Fatal.

FLEDGE: Sounds like you're threatening me, Mr Dawlish.

DAWLISH: Does it? I can get into your head and come out with your secrets dangling on the end of my nose ...

FLEDGE: I know that, Mr Dawlish.

DAWLISH: So. No message from Slatterthwaite.

FLEDGE: I think he wants to take you on. I warned him.

DAWLISH: You did right. I could almost admire him for that.

FLEDGE: There was one thing.

DAWLISH: Oh?

FLEDGE: He went to see Teddy Hilton.

DAWLISH: Ah.

FLEDGE: He's dead, Mr Dawlish. Last night. The home help found him. He said he was ill. He thought he was dying ... I didn't believe him either. Poor devil ...

DAWLISH: How very inconvenient.

FLEDGE: Inconvenient?

DAWLISH: To go like that before he could tell his little sad story.

FLEDGE: I suppose so.

DAWLISH: Advantage Slatterthwaite. So what do we do now? To suggest?

FLEDGE	Actually Mr Dawlish I was going to ask if I could be released from duties.
DAWLISH	Well, well. Celia spot on again.
FLEDGE	Celia?
DAWLISH	She said you wouldn't last. Intuition. Her strong point. Unfortunately for her it isn't quite enough. I've had to find a replacement. Not only have I lost interest bodywise but Celia, you see, has been blabbing. I'm hoping for better things from the new one. Julie-Anne. I never give up hope, you see. Why do you want to leave?
FLEDGE	I don't think it's quite my line of work.
DAWLISH	I expected loyalty.
FLEDGE	I'm sorry. I just feel I've done all I can.
DAWLISH	Shall I tell you what the trouble with you is, you're soft. In these difficult times it's important to know whose side you're on. You're shaking, look at you.
FLEDGE	Sorry. I—
DAWLISH	Look at your hands. D'you know I think that's conscience. I'm working towards its abolition, did you know that? A splendid concept don't you think? A lot of work is being done in that field . . . a little joke Fledge.
FLEDGE	I'll work out the rest of the week. On the cars.
DAWLISH	You won't. You're released. As of now. How unfortunate.
FLEDGE	I . . . I'm not a blabber Mr Dawlish.
DAWLISH	On the other hand, you're not a deaf and dumb fish in my tank, are you? Even if at this moment you'd like to be. But then there's nothing to blab is there?
FLEDGE	I . . . no.
DAWLISH	Nothing to hide. Nothing . . . unfinished?
	Silence.
DAWLISH	You're leaving at a crucial moment, Fledge. Things are being done. Not just by me. There are others. I'll say goodnight then. By the way, if you want a reference you can always contact me. You know where to find me, Fledge, and I you. Goodnight now.
	Door closed.

FLEDGE	(*narrates*) I slept badly. Dreams scurried loose in my head like rats. Dreams of footsteps behind me on the pavement, figures in waiting cars from black and white childhood movies, whispered phone calls. I woke up early and peered out at an ordinary September sky over an ordinary suburb. I watched a milk float clanking down the empty street and for the first time in my life I felt like leaving the city forever. I stayed in my house for three days. The phone didn't ring, no-one knocked at the door. The weekend was a blank. Then on Monday morning I went into the city centre. A Wimpy bar near the library, I chose a corner seat and watched the doorway. Dawlish was right. My hands were shaking. I was a deserter and I knew what they did to them ...
	A Wimpy bar—muzak.
JOE	Fledge ...
	A coffee cup is spilled.
FLEDGE	Hell ...
JOE	Steady.
FLEDGE	Sorry. Joe. How are you? Still backing favourites?
JOE	Jumpy, aren't you?
FLEDGE	I was miles away.
JOE	You look poorly.
FLEDGE	I have been a bit off. Out of action for a few days.
JOE	It'll be this virus whatsit. I heard some doctor bloke on about it on the local radio. It's a new strain. Everybody's got it. Or will have. He knew it all. What about the news, then?
FLEDGE	What?
JOE	The Slatterthwaite business.
FLEDGE	What about him?
JOE	He's been beaten up. Mugged. Going home from a council meeting. It's been in the papers. TV. The lot.
FLEDGE	How bad is it?
JOE	He's in a coma. Intensive care and all that. Rumour is he'll not get better. Paralysed. Finito. Have you really not

heard? Bastard kids. Mind, no-one's safe, are they. I don't go out after about seven o'clock. Not worth it. I've got this far. The Nazis and the teddy boys didn't get me, and I'm not going to let some skinhead-punks spoil the record. You were asking after him, weren't you? Meet him, did you?

FLEDGE   We were mates. It goes back a long time. Yes I saw him.

JOE   They haven't caught anybody. Do they ever? What about Rovers, then? Won six-nil. Morisco got a hat-trick. Foreigners. Remember when we won the cup in 1934. I went to Wembley. First time I'd ever been to London. I can remember the team. Morris, Crane, Brocklehurst, Jessop, Waring, Mappin, Webb, Walker, Hall, Burton and May. They were all local lads. And another thing since you've been out of the swim, Dickinson's has closed. No more 'chocky' buttons. First it was all the factories. Now with Dickinson's gone the bloody city won't be on the map soon will it? Nobody'll be able to remember why we're all living here in the first place!! See you, Fledgey. Hope you feel better soon ... it'll be this bug ... like I say. By the way, the scissor sharpening's going all right. I'll have no hair left soon ...

Fade up life-support machine bleep—a hospital side ward.

FLEDGE   (*narrates*) The hospital. Like Hilton said. That sweet smell of talcum. Whispers round the beds at visiting time. Green screens around bits of pain. It was like before, with Kath. A face on the pillow staring up waiting to come back in.

NURSE   I'm afraid you can't stay long. Mr Slatterthwaite's in no state really. I shouldn't let you in. You can stay for a few moments. He can't talk of course.

FLEDGE   (*narrates*) I leaned close. The blocked mind struggled. He stared into me and on and past. I had the sudden feeling that this moment was where I had been travelling to for a long long time. And here I was. I leaned closer.

SLATTER-   (*Whisper*) I saw him ... Fledge. Balaclava ... smiling
THWAITE   ... the fist ... on here ... Mick ... Mick ... on here ... I told him ... it doesn't have to be like this ... I told him ... it doesn't have to be like this.

Support machine gives long warning bleep.

NURSE   Stand outside please.

FLEDGE I—

NURSE   Quickly please!

Cut.

FLEDGE (*narrates*) Outside the swish of rain on the dark pavements, the hum of traffic. The city. Sullen. Grey. Widowed in the November rain. Crisp as lace in the May sunshine. Empty as an echo on Sundays and at night sharp as a razor and sometimes dangerous. And the people. The woman on the bus checking the locks on her doors for the third time as Tamsin tries hard for Oxbridge; Celia alone in her flat in front of the mirror; Joe Brackenbury making the most of a couple of brown ales in front of an evening's telly; the 'anything' girl from the park sat among the gleaming portables waiting for the yellow-smile boy; the Town Hall commissionaire neat as a nail heading for the usual in his local pub; Kennedy in his bungalow on a nice road where the cars wait like sentries in the driveways; Kamikazi Sam rooting the streets for left-overs; the headmaster, the barmaid, the taxi-driver, the suitcase man with the necklaces flashing in the last of the summer sun. And Kramer going south and the 'Krugerrand Kid' smiling in another country and the chocolate button women blowing their final wage packet and Duggie in his red top-hat on the club steps and all the girls in the streaming city streets in their regatta hats; and the boy Mick smiling at midnight... the alsatian at the gate, the gun in the drawer... the fist in the face. And Eric Slatterthwaite, up for an O.B.E. if times had only been different, suddenly a dark bundle on a midnight pavement and now at a breathless frail ending in the white hospital bed where the machine stops.. And Dawlish, all alone in his windowless office, puts the phone down on another deal, swivels in his chair and turns out the light. In two and a half minutes in his best car he'll be in the city centre which awaits him now, this the coming man. I crossed the road by the post office and watched from a doorway as the white-faced boy in the trench coat pocketed his loose change, packed up his guitar and headed for the dark night.

Music to finish.

THREADS

Barry Hines

THREADS was first broadcast by BBC 2 on 23 September 1984. The cast was as follows:

Ruth Beckett	KAREN MEAGHER
Jimmy Kemp	REECE DINSDALE
Mr Kemp	DAVID BRIERLEY
Mrs Kemp	RITA MAY
Michael Kemp	NICHOLAS LANE
Alison Kemp	JANE HAZLEGROVE
Mr Beckett	HENRY MOXON
Mrs Beckett	JUNE BROUGHTON
Granny Beckett	SYLVIA STOKER
Mr Sutton	HARRY BEETY
Mrs Sutton	RUTH HOLDEN
Bob	ASHLEY BARKER
Chief Supt. Hirst	MICHAEL O'HAGAN
Medical Officer	PHIL ROSE
Information Officer	STEVE HALLIWELL
Accommodation Officer	BRIAN GRELLIS
Transport Officer	PETER FAULKNER
Food Officer	ANTHONY COLLIN
Scientific Advisor	MICHAEL ELY
Manpower Officer	SHARON BAYLIS
Works Officer	DAVID STUTT
Mr Stothard	PHIL ASKHAM
Mrs Stothard	ANNA SEYMOUR
Carol Stothard	FIONA ROOK
Woman in Supermarket	CHRISTINE BUCKLEY
Shopkeeper	JOE BELCHER
Boy in Supermarket	DAVID MAJOR
Peace Speaker	MAGGIE FORD
Trade Unionist	MIKE KAY
Officer at Food Depot	RICHARD ALBRECHT
Policemen	TED BEYER
	DEAN WILLIAMSON
Mr Langley	JOE HOLMES
Patrol Officer	ANDY FENN-RODGERS
1st Soldier	GRAHAM HILL
2nd Soldier	NIGEL COLLINS
Looters	JERRY READY
Woman at Hospital	GRETA DUNN
Old Man in Graveyard	NAT JACKLEY
Street Trader	JOHN LIVESEY
Stunt Double Mrs Kemp	DOROTHY FORD
Newscasters	LESLEY JUDD
	COLIN WARD-LEWIS
Narrator	PAUL VAUGHAN
Jane	VICTORIA O'KEEFE
Spike	LEE DALEY
Gaz	MARCUS LUND

Produced and directed by MICK JACKSON

Titles

> *In close-up, a single, horizontal thread, backlit against a darker background. The camera pans along it. It is joined to a vertical crossthread, then to another ... We are looking at the fine detail of a British woodland spider's web. It moves gently in a breeze.*

COMMENTARY In an urban society, everything connects. Each person's needs are fed by the skills of many others. Our lives are woven together in a fabric. But the connections that make society strong also make it vulnerable.

> *Beyond the web, as if seen from a hillside, is a distant view of the city of Sheffield. Steam and smoke rise from the steelworks. The sun's reflection glints on the windows and roofs of the city's traffic. It is a bright spring day.*
>
> *Title: 'THREADS' by Barry Hines.*

1. Exterior. A hill outside Sheffield. Afternoon.

> *Caption: 'Sheffield, Saturday March 5th'.*
>
> *There is a shattering roar as a military aircraft passes low overhead. A solitary car is parked on the edge of an outcrop of rock overlooking the view. There are two people sitting in the front seats.*
>
> *Inside the car, the radio is on, playing rock music.* JIMMY *who is in his twenties, is sitting in the driver's seat, smoking.* RUTH, *his girlfriend and a year or two younger, is sitting beside him. Below them, in the distance, they can see the city where they both live and where they have just driven from. There is no-one else in sight. They sit looking out of the window for a few seconds without speaking. It is a Saturday afternoon.*

RUTH	Peaceful up here, isn't it (*Rather sheepishly,* JIMMY *turns down the radio*). Oh, I'd love to live out in the country. Wouldn't you Jimmy?
JIMMY	Would I heck.
RUTH	Why not?
JIMMY	It's dead. There's nothing to do. Just imagine living down there. It'd take you an hour to get to nearest boozer.
RUTH	Oh, I know, but the air's lovely. (*She winds down the window, inhales extravagantly, then winds the window up again*). Do you know, I love it this time of the year when spring's coming on. Look, see the leaves just coming out on that bush over there. (JIMMY *is taking no notice of her, staring out of the window*). What are you looking at?
JIMMY	I'm trying to make out where our house is. I wish I'd a pair of binoculars. You can see the floodlights at the United ground, look ... (*The mention of the football reminds him of something*). What time is it? The half-time scores will be on in a minute!
	He begins to turn the dial of the radio, pausing briefly at several stations as he tries to find the correct one. Snatches of an assortment of programmes can be heard, including a news bulletin which mentions rumours of a crisis in Iran. We hear no details, as JIMMY *passes on to the next station. He finds what he is looking for just in time to hear the half-time progress reports on the local teams*
RUTH	Honestly! We come out here for a drive, we're surrounded by all this beautiful countryside, and all you can think about is football.
JIMMY	(*grinnning and putting an arm round* RUTH). It's not all I think about.
RUTH	Stop it! Honestly, you've no consideration at all sometimes. You think you can do what you like. (JIMMY *gets out of the car*). Where are you going?
	A few seconds later, JIMMY *gets back into the car. He is holding a few sprigs of heather, which he presents to* RUTH.

JIMMY	There you are. Peace offering. Not much smell to it, though.
RUTH	It's lovely.
JIMMY	Heather's supposed to bring good luck, isn't it?
RUTH	That's what they say.
JIMMY	I wonder if it'll bring me any?

He puts his arm round RUTH *and this time, still holding the heather, she responds,* JIMMY *gently pushes her down into her seat, as she lets the heather fall to the ground.*

Cut to a very wide shot. Their car is seen on a rocky precipice as the radio continues and fades.

2. Interior. A pub in Sheffield. Evening.

Caption: 'Thursday May 5th'.

At the far end of the bar is a TV set tuned to the early evening news. No-one in the pub is paying much attention to it. Newsfilm is on the televison. The camerawork is shaky.

NEWSREADER *(Speaking over the newsfilm)* This film, shot secretly by a West German television crew on Tuesday, shows one of the Soviet convoys on the move in northern Iran. The convoys were first spotted by United States satellites on Monday moving across three of the mountain passes leading from the Soviet Union. The Soviet Foreign Minister has defended the incursions and has accused the United States of deliberately prompting last week's coup in Iran... Speaking on his arrival in Vienna, Mr Gromyko claimed the Soviet vehicles responded to appeals from the legitimate government forces...

The news bulletin continues faintly throughout the scene. In the pub JIMMY *and* RUTH *sit at a table in earnest conversation.* RUTH *has just discovered she is pregnant.*

JIMMY   You being serious?

RUTH	Course I'm being serious. I've never been more serious in my life. What we gonna do, Jimmy... Jimmy?
JIMMY	Well, are you sure?
RUTH	Not definitely, but I'm normally as regular as clockwork. Anyway, what if I am? It's not the end of the world is it?

We see the TV, showing the BBC symbol on it.

ANNOUNCER	And now a look at programmes later this evening on BBC1...

3. Exterior. The pub. Evening

We see the lights at the windows and in the foreground the evening traffic passes. Over this, the signature tune of a TV programme: 'Tomorrow's World'.

4. Exterior. Newsagent's Day.

Caption: 'Sunday, May 8th'.

The newsagent is writing numbers on the Sunday papers, which carry the headline 'Moscow hits back at U.S. stage management'. JIMMY's sister, ALISON KEMP (16), is reading a magazine and wearing headphones for a Walkman.

NEWSAGENT	And don't forget number twenty-four today.
ALISON	*(lifting headphones)* What?
NEWSAGENT	I said, don't forget number twenty-four today. You're gonna ruin your hearing with those things on all the time, you know.

5. Exterior. Documentary Footage.

Wide shot of tanks moving along in convoy.

6. Exterior. Back of the Kemps' house. Evening.

Wide shot of the back yard of a modern council house on a small estate. We hear the banging of pans from inside.

7. Interior. The Kemps' house. Evening

>JIMMY *and his other, who works in a clothing factory, are sitting at the table waiting for their evening meal to be served.* MR KEMP *who is on the dole, is in the adjoining kitchen preparing it.* MICHAEL *(9) is sitting on the hearthrug playing with a pocket battery game.* MRS KEMP *is still wearing her overall from work.* MR KEMP *is wearing an apron.* JIMMY *has just told them about Ruth's pregnancy and the atmosphere between the three adults is tense.* MICHAEL *carries on playing as if nothing has happened.* MR KEMP *shows his displeasure by banging the pans about as he prepares the meal.*

MR KEMP (*shouting through from the kitchen*) Honestly, Jimmy, you want your bloody head seeing to!

MRS KEMP I think he wants something else seeing to as well.

JIMMY Don't blame me. It's not my fault.

MR KEMP Whose fault is it then, you daft bugger?

MRS KEMP Don't go blaming it all on Ruth, Jimmy, that's not fair.

>MR KEMP *comes through from the kitchen carrying two plates of lamb chops, chips and peas which he places before* JIMMY *and his mother.*

MR KEMP Anyway, it's irrelevant who's to blame now. Here you are, luv. The point is, what are you going to do about it?

JIMMY We're going to get married.

>MRS KEMP *looks up at her husband.*

MR KEMP What for?

JIMMY (*taken aback by the question*). Because we want to, what do you think?

MRS KEMP You don't have to, you know, Jimmy. I wouldn't want you to think that we were pushing you into it.

JIMMY Nobody's pushing us into nowt. It's what we want. We've decided.

MRS KEMP I suppose you've talked about an abortion?

JIMMY (*agitated*) Of course we have, but neither of us want that. We want to get married and have the baby.

MICHAEL (*looking up from his game*) Mum, what's that mean abortion?

MR KEMP Michael!

MRS KEMP Never mind what it means. You get on with your game. It's nothing to do with you.

MICHAEL *resumes his game without further inquiry.*

JIMMY We were thinking of getting engaged anyway, so it doesn't make much difference really. It's just brought it forward a bit, that's all.

MR KEMP I hope you know what you're doing, Jimmy. It's a hell of a time to be starting a family in the middle of a recession.

ALISON *enters the room, brushing her hair, and then sees* MICHAEL *playing.*

ALISON What are you doing with that?

MICHAEL I'm not hurting it.

ALISON *walks to the mirror.*

MICHAEL Our Jimmy's getting married!

ALISON Are you?

JIMMY I might be. Why?

ALISON Well, it's a bit sudden, isn't it? You're not even engaged.

JIMMY How do you know? Anyway, it's nothing to do with you, so keep your nose out.

ALISON Are you getting married in church or in a registry office?

MICHAEL Alison, what's an abortion?

MRS KEMP Michael! I've told you once.

ALISON Oh, so *that's* it.

MRS KEMP	I'll give you a good hiding, lad, if you don't keep your mouth shut.
MICHAEL	What for? I haven't done anything yet.
MR KEMP	Are you going to shut up about it?
	JIMMY *gets up angrily, storms into the kitchen and slams the door.*
MRS KEMP	I hope you two are both satisfied now.
ALISON	What are you blaming *me* for? *I* haven't done anything wrong.

MICHAEL *has gone back to his pocket battery game.*

8. Exterior. Kemps' garden. Evening.

It is a few minutes later. JIMMY *is in the aviary, feeding his birds. He has calmed down and speaking quietly to them, trying to get them to have some grain. We hear the sound of a radio broadcast over this.*

RADIO NEWSCASTER	The time now, seven thirty. Douglas Barton with tonight's headlines.
	The United States has hinted it may send troops to the Middle East if the Russians don't move their forces out of Iran.
	The Prime Minister has joined the chorus of Western leaders calling for immediate withdrawal and has spoken of 'a serious threat to world peace'.
	Four people were killed today on the M6 motorway in Staffordshire when their car was in collision with a heavy tanker. The accident happened at the junction with the A449 near Dunston.

9. Documentary footage. Day.

Wide shot of industrial chimneys.

Caption: 'Sheffield. Fourth largest city in Britain. Population 545,000'.

Cut to melting shop of a steelworks, full of smoke, fire and steam, men working.

Caption: 'Main industries: Steel, Engineering, Chemicals'.

10. Interior. Steelworks. Day.

Close-up of a man we do not yet recognize, his face lit by the red glow of the hot steel. He is wearing a suit and a hard hat. It is MR BECKETT, *a departmental manager at the steelworks.*

Caption: 'Nearest Military Targets: NATO air base, RAF communications centre'.

11. Exterior. Beckett's house. Day.

Caption: 'Wednesday May 11th'.

RUTH's *house is a comfortable Victorian semi in the western suburbs of the city. A woman's face is looking out from behind net curtains. This is* MRS BECKETT, RUTH's *mother.*

Inside the house, RUTH *is sitting on a sofa, stroking the cat.*

MRS BECKETT   Do you think we'll get on alright?

RUTH   I can't see why not. They're ever so nice.

MR BECKETT enters the room and walks across to turn on the television. He is the man we saw earlier at the steelworks.

MRS BECKETT   I just wish we'd been meeting in different circumstances, that's all.

RUTH   You're making it sound like a funeral.

MRS BECKETT   It's embarrassing though, isn't it? It ought to have been a happy occasion.

RUTH   It is a happy occasion. (*Defiantly*) Well, I'm happy anyway.

MRS BECKETT I must say, it's brought out a very determined streak in you, has this...

MR BECKETT puts down the newspaper he was reading in order to watch the television news. On the television we see, briefly, a correspondent live from Washington. MR BECKETT *watches intently, while* RUTH *and* MRS BECKETT *ignore it. The correspondent's words continue in the background through the next few moments of the scene. Although we can hardly hear him, this is what he's saying:*

NEWS CORRESPDT On a day that has seen U.S. Naval forces in the Indian Ocean put on high alert, and on the eve of the Iran debate in the Security Council, this morning's report in the Washington Post came as a bombshell to most Americans. Quoting 'sources close to the Administration', the Washington Post says that there has been a serious incident involving a United States warship in the waters off the coast of Iran. No further details are given in the story attributed to the paper's Defence Correspondent. However, one rumour being heard increasingly in the Capitol this morning says that the vessel is a United States submarine that has disappeared while on routine patrol in the area. Coming just at the same time, the latest news of a Naval alert has alarmed many people by seeming to confirm that something very serious has happened. A Pentagon spokesman has refused to be drawn one way or the other on the crisis, parrying all reporters' questions at his regular morning press briefing.

Meanwhile, outside, THE KEMPS *are arriving.*

MRS BECKETT It looks as if they're here.

She begins to plump up cushions, and checks her appearance in the mirror, obscuring MR BECKETT's *view of the television as she does so.*

MRS BECKETT Didn't you hear what I said, Gordon? Mr and Mrs Kemp are here.

RUTH *has moved to the window. She exchanges glances with* JIMMY *as the Kemp family approach the house.*

MRS BECKETT Well, come on then, turn the television off. You can't watch that while they're here.

> MR BECKETT *crosses slowly and reluctantly to the television. The doorbell rings, and in the hall* MRS BECKETT *greets her visitors as they enter.*

MRS BECKETT Do come in. Do come in.

RUTH Mum, Mrs Kemp, Mr Kemp.

MRS BECKETT How do you do?

MR & MRS KEMP Pleased to meet you.

> MR BECKETT *has appeared at the doorway leading from the hall.*

RUTH Dad, Mr and Mrs Kemp.

MRS BECKETT Do go through.

MR & MRS KEMP Thank you.

> *They all file into the front room as* MRS BECKETT *closes the front door.*

12. Exterior. Newsagent's. Day.

Caption: 'Thursday May 12th'.

As ALISON *comes out of the shop to collect her bicycle, we hear the radio news.*

NEWSCASTER BBC News at 8 o'clock. The Soviet Union has protested strongly to the United States about what it calls 'dangerous provocations' by American warships in the Gulf of Oman yesterday. This follows an incident in which serious damage was caused to the Soviet cruiser 'Kirov' when she was in collision with the U.S. destroyer 'Callaghan'.

13. Empty flat. Day.

JIMMY (*taps the walls and pulls up some pieces of lino*) It's in a bit of a state, but it's got possibilities.

RUTH	I'd like the door stripped down ... all this paper off ... and the walls white.
JIMMY	It looks as if there's about sixteen layers on here.
RUTH	My mother and dad will help us, I'm sure they will.
JIMMY	(*inspects the woodwork and jumps up and down on the floorboards*) My dad will give us a hand as well. He'll be glad of something to do.
RUTH	What are you laughing at?
JIMMY	I'm just thinking of his face when my mother said that we could borrow his redundancy money. I think he was fancying a trip to Bermuda on it. It looks like being Blackpool again.
RUTH	I like the gardens. I think it's lovely for the children to have somewhere to play.
JIMMY	I wonder if they'll let me build an aviary down there.
RUTH	You and your birds.
JIMMY	Makes you feel funny, though, don't it?
RUTH	What do you mean?
JIMMY	The thought of owning a home. Being married. Having children. It's enough to put years on you, isn't it?
RUTH	Don't be silly (*She puts her arms around* JIMMY's *neck*). It'll be lovely. I just know it will.

14. Exterior. Sheffield. Night.

A wide shot of Sheffield at night, with many lights. On the soundtrack, Debussy's 'Clair de lune'.

15. Interior. Kemps' living room. Night.

A girl's hand copies a French exercise into a schoolbook. It is ALISON, *doing her homework. A TV is on in the background, but* ALISON *ignores it: she is wearing stereo headphones. A glass of milk is put on the table.*

MRS KEMP   Here you are, luv.
ALISON   *(looks up)* Ta.

She takes note of the TV, which can be heard only faintly at first, drowned out by the music from her headphones.

TV
CORRESPDT   ... American and Israeli search and rescue vessels in the area today came across debris and oil slicks that can only have come from the missing submarine. It is still being said in Washington that the 'Los Angeles' was on a routine reconnaissance mission off the coast of Iran when she sank last Tuesday with the loss of all hands.

ALISON takes off her headphones. As she does so, the music fades down and the TV sound comes up. She drinks her milk.

TV
CORRESPDT   After paying tribute to her 127 officers and men, the President went on to say that he held the Soviet Union solely responsible for their deaths and for the vessel's disappearance.

AMERICAN
VOICE   The unprovoked attack on our submarine and the move into Iran are the actions of a reckless and warlike power. I have to warn the Soviets, in the clearest possible terms, that they risk taking us to the brink of an armed confrontation—with incalculable consequences for all mankind.

16. Exterior. Sheffield Town Hall. Day.

COMMENTARY   Britain has emergency plans for war. If Central Government should ever fail, power can be transferred instead to a system of local officials dispersed across the country.

Cut to CLIVE SUTTON, *the City Chief Executive, watering some plants in the offices.*

In an urban district like Sheffield there is already a designated wartime controller—he's the city's peacetime Chief executive. If it should suddenly become necessary, he can be given full powers of internal government.

Cut back to external shots of Sheffield.

Threads   171

When or if this happens depends on the crisis itself.

17. Exterior. Sheffield. Day.

Caption: 'Tuesday May 17th'.

Images of Sheffield town centre, and the industrial chimneys. Then, in close-up, on the front page of a 'Daily Telegraph' there is the headline, 'U.S. Acts on Iran'. It is MR BECKETT who is reading it. Men are passing him on their way to work.

A series of images: parachutes in the sky, as if on a news bulletin; JIMMY working in a joinery; news footage of U.S. marines coming off aircraft; RUTH opening a tin of cat food.

Over these images we hear an American voice. It is that of a State Department spokesman.

AMERICAN VOICE   The United States Government has been forced— reluctantly—to take action to safeguard what it believes are legitimate Western interests in the Middle East.

This administration has therefore resolved to send units of its rapid deployment force, the U.S. Central Command, into western Iran. We are confident that the Soviet Union will take note of our resolve not to be intimidated and will desist from its present, perilous course of action.

18. Interior. Various.

A piece of headed note paper is in a typewriter. The heading reads 'Home Office, Queen Anne's Gate, London SW1H 9AT'. As the carriage moves we see that it is addressed to 'Mr C. Sutton, Town Hall, Sheffield'. Of the text, we can see only a few phrases which read '... authorities are requested to undertake an initial review of the emergency arrangements ... does not cause undue public alarm or concern...'.

Cut to close-up of MICHAEL making a model aeroplane and

playing with it. In the background the football results can be heard.

Cut back to a wide shot of the typing pool where the letter is being typed.

19. Interior. Mr Sutton's office. Day.

A POLICE MOTORCYCLIST *has just handed* MR SUTTON *a letter. The envelope is marked in red 'Secret—Eyes of Addressee Only'.*

MOTORCYCLIST Thank you very much sir.

MR SUTTON Thank you.

The motorcyclist salutes and leaves the room.

MR SUTTON *sits at his desk, reading the letter. He unlocks a desk drawer, and takes out a folder marked 'War Book Vol. 1'.*

In the outer office, Mr Sutton's SECRETARY *is chatting quietly over a cup of tea with the* POLICE MOTORCYCLIST. *The buzzer on the telephone goes, and she picks it up.*

SECRETARY Hello.

MR SUTTON Mary, I want you to contact the following people and have them in my office in ten minutes time. I don't care what they're doing. They're to drop it and get here right away. Is that clear? Right. Got a pencil? O.K.

Alan Bolton... George Cox... Roger Fisher... Susan Russell... Yes, administration... Tony Barnes... Rod Chamberlain...

As he reads we cut to a close-up of the list, which designates these people's emergency functions.

20. Interior. Small Supermarket. Day.

The supermarket is busy, even though it is only midweek. MRS KEMP, *shopping on her way home from work, is standing in one of the long queues. She looks around the shop, slight concern showing on her face.*

MRS KEMP   It's busy for a Wednesday, isn't it? You'd think it was Christmas.

21. Documentary footage.

Troops running across tarmac.

Caption: 'Thursday May 19th'.

Interior. Mr Sutton's office. Day.

MR SUTTON *is at his desk, speaking into the telephone. His* SECRETARY *is pouring him tea as he speaks. In the background the weather forecast is on the radio.*

MR SUTTON   And what about the food situation? What've we got?... And what about flour?... What else is there?... Corned beef! I hope it's not from Argentina... O.K.... What about supplies for first aid posts?... Is that all? Well that's not going to get us very far, is it?... What? ... Well, I'm sure I don't know, if I'm honest. We've heard nothing about Emergency Powers as yet. Anyway, don't make a song and dance about it, just get on with it. Don't tell anyone you don't have to, eh. O.K.

He replaces the telephone.

23. Exterior. Primary school, Sheffield. Later that day.

It is break time at the school, and the children are out in the playground. A van is parked outside a side door, and the driver is unloading bundles of blankets. A crowd of children have stopped playing and are watching the operation silently. MICHAEL KEMP *is among the watching children.*

24. Exterior. Allotments. Early evening.

JIMMY *dressed up ready to go out, gets out of his car and walks down the hill towards his father's allotment. It is a fine early summer evening, and he passes other people working on their plots. Over this pleasant, relaxed scene, we hear a news announcement.*

NEWSCASTER The remaining units of the United States 10th Airborne Division, which parachuted into western Iran yesterday, have taken up defensive positions near Isfahan designed, according to the spokesman, to block any possible move towards the oilfields in the Persian Gulf.

Squadrons of American B-52 bombers have been arriving at U.S. bases in Turkey since late on Tuesday evening, together with three AWACS early warning aircraft. It's believed that they'll be used in a supporting role to the Middle East Task Force.

MR KEMP, who is planting potatoes, sees JIMMY approaching and looks up.

MR KEMP Alright then?

Some pigeons fly out of a loft. As JIMMY looks over to the loft, A MAN appears and acknowledges him.

JIMMY Alright John?

MR KEMP Come to give me a hand, then?

JIMMY No chance, I've done enough for one day. I'm knackered.

MR KEMP Not too knackered to be going out though I see.

JIMMY That's different, isn't it? Anyway, I need a break, I've been down at the house every night this week.

MR KEMP How's it coming on?

JIMMY Not too bad. We're just trying to get the living room and bedroom finished before we move in.

With a shattering roar, an RAF Phantom flies over. They both stop and look up at it.

JIMMY Mother says will you take some flowers down when you've finished.

Mr Kemp's friend JOHN is still at the doorway of his loft. MR KEMP turns to him.

MR KEMP Third since tea-time.

JOHN Aye.

JIMMY	Where are they going to?
MR KEMP	Finningley, I suppose.
JIMMY	Why don't you pop into W.H. Smith's and buy yourself an aircraft spotter's book? You could start a new hobby. It'd make a change from gardening.
MR KEMP	You can laugh, but there's something going on, I'm telling you.
JIMMY	There'll be something going on tonight when I've had a few pints.
MR KEMP	Don't be going mad. You've not only yourself to think about now, you know.
JIMMY	Why not? I might as well enjoy myself while I'm single. I've not long to go now, you know.
MR KEMP	Yes, you could be right there.

25. Documentary footage.

Caption: 'RAF Finningley. Likely Wartime function: base for U.S. Phantom jets'.

A plane is on a runway. A vehicle moves through the gates.

Caption: '5 miles from Doncaster, 17 miles from Sheffield'.

The base's alert status board has the heading 'BIKINI STATE'. A hand takes out the slate saying 'BLACK' and replaces it with a slate saying 'AMBER'.

26. Interior. Pub. Evening of the same day.

JIMMY and BOB, his mate from work, are in a pub in town. They have both had a few drinks. The pub is noisy. A juke box is playing 'Johnnie Be Good'. The television is on behind the bar showing the Nine O'Clock News.

JIMMY	I'll have a half.
BOB	Half! What's up with you? Getting into training for when you're married?

BOB *goes to the bar with the empty glasses, grinning at two pretty girls who are sitting at the other end of the pub.*

BOB Two bitters in them please. Cheers.

JIMMY is looking up at the television behind the bar, straining to hear what is being said. We are aware of other heads glancing towards the set.

NEWSREADER In a statement issued a short time ago by the Pentagon in Washington, the United States has accused the Soviet Union of moving nuclear warheads into their new base at Mashad in Northern Iran. According to the American spokesman...

The bar has gone noticeably quieter. The LANDLORD noticing the change, looks up, misinterprets the silence and switches channels.

JIMMY Hey! I was watching that!

There are similar protests from other parts of the pub. The LANDLORD switches it back to the news.

NEWSREADER ...aboard two giant Antonov transport planes late yesterday afternoon and were immediately moved under cover into temporary hangers...

BOB comes back with the drinks.

JIMMY See that? I was just watching that about the Far East and he goes and turns it over.

BOB Far East? Why, what's going on there?

JIMMY Iran. The Americans have just said the Russians...

BOB Iran! That's not the Far East you pillock! That's the Middle East. China and Hong Kong. *That's* the Far East.

JIMMY So what? It's far enough, isn't it?

BOB I'd sooner go the near east myself, Scarborough and Skegness.

JIMMY Skeggy! I'd sooner watch my toenails grow than go there.

BOB	Anyway, never mind that rubbish. What about these two birds to east of this table?

He indicates the girls at the other end of the room. JIMMY *takes no notice of him.*

JIMMY	My dad's right, you know. It's getting serious.
BOB	There's nothing we can do about it, is there? We might as well enjoy ourselves while we can.
JIMMY	I know, but doesn't it scare you, what it might lead to?
BOB	'Course it bloody scares me. But there's nought we can do about it, is there? And I'll tell you one thing, if a bomb does drop I want to be pissed out my mind and straight underneath it when it happens.

They glance back towards the television. The programme's Diplomatic Correspondent is now analysing the implications of the news item.

CORRESPDT	... which means neither side can back down. Arriving here in Brussels a short time ago, NATO's Secretary General said...

BOB *nudges* JIMMY, *trying to shake him out of his thoughtful mood.*

BOB	Come on, you miserable bugger. It's all these family responsibilities. You're acting like a married man already.
JIMMY	It'll not be long now.
BOB	You'd better make the best of it then, hadn't you, while you've still chance? What about chatting these two birds up then?
JIMMY	I can't do that.
BOB	Come on. It might be the last chance you get. Anyway, if we are going to cop it, we might as well go out with a bang, that's what I say.

BOB *gets up with his beer and* JIMMY, *laughing, follows him.*

JIMMY   There can't be many better ways of going I don't suppose, blown up on the job.

They walk towards the two girls. On the television the news continues.

NEWSREADER   ...and we've just heard that the Prime Minister has issued a message of support for the United States government. The statement, just released from Downing Street, condemns what it calls 'reckless Soviet action which can only worsen an already grave situation'.

We cut to an exterior shot of the Town Hall at night. One light is on in an upstairs window.

27. Interior. Mr Sutton's office. Night.

MR SUTTON *working late. He is using a calculator and there are piles of paper on his desk, which is lit by a single lamp. He picks up the microphone of a tape recorder and speaks into it.*

MR SUTTON   To the Director, Technical Services. Please let me know what fuel stocks are currently held in each depot. Please ensure that tanks are kept topped up and that no fuel is used except for essential works only.

28. Exterior. Layby. Night.

It is two hours after the pub scene. JIMMY's car is parked in a layby. Everything is quiet, then there is the rumble of approaching traffic and a long convoy of heavy vehicles goes by. The noise disturbs the occupants of the car and JIMMY's face appears at the back window, wiping the steam to see what is going on. One of the girls we saw in the pub also appears. The two faces remain framed in the back window.

29. Exterior. Sheffield. Day.

Caption: 'Saturday May 21st'.

Various shots of Sheffield town centre. Over this we hear a newsreader.

NEWSCASTER   There's been no response from the Soviet Government a yet to the United States' ultimatum, delivered to Moscow last night. The American note calls for joint withdrawal of all U.S. and Soviet forces from Iran by noon on Sunday.

However, NATO observers in West Germany have reported increasing buildups of Warsaw Pact troops and vehicles at points along the central frontier this morning.

Cut to news footage of troops embarking onto a plane.

The Ministry of Defence has announced it's sending more troops to Europe to reinforce the British commitment to NATO. The first contingents left RAF Brize Norton this morning.

30. Exterior. Sheffield town centre. Day.

A crowd moves through the streets on a CND march for peace. The marchers are chanting and waving banners, and there is a police presence.

JIMMY and RUTH are coming out of Mothercare as the marchers pass them, and they stop to watch.

Over this, the newscaster's voice.

NEWSCASTER   The day has been marked by a number of demonstrations up and down the country, reflecting support for and against the Government's decision to reinforce Europe. Although most of these passed off without incident, police made a number of arrests for disorderly conduct at rallies in the North and Midlands.

31. Documentary footage.

Shots of British Airways jets parked at Heathrow airport, and of stranded passengers.

NEWSCASTER   The Government has taken control of British Airways and all cross-channel ferries. They say it's a temporary step to help move troops to Europe. Thousands are stranded at Heathrow and Gatwick.

Shot of an oil-drilling platform in the North Sea.

And the Royal Navy is to guard the North Sea oil rigs. The M.O.D. says it's a 'prudent precautionary measure'.

32. Exterior. The newsagent's. Day.

Caption: 'Sunday May 22nd'.

ALISON KEMP *comes out of the newsagent's shop with a bag of papers. She has a news round. She collects her bicycle and disappears up the road.*

33. Exterior. Centre of Sheffield. Day.

A large-scale anti-war rally. A WOMAN SPEAKER *is addressing the crowd, amongst which is* RUTH, *from the steps of the City Hall.*

WOMAN SPEAKER This time they are playing with, at best, the destruction of life as we know it, and at worst total annihilation. You cannot win a nuclear war!

There is cheering and jeering from the crowd.

Now, just suppose the Russians win this war. What would they be winning? Well, I'll tell you. All major centres of population and industry will have been destroyed...

VOICE FROM CROWD Industry? What industry? We ain't got no industry in Sheffield.

WOMAN SPEAKER Yes, and if...

She is drowned out by the crowd's laughter and shouting.

VOICE FROM CROWD They'd be wasting a bomb on it.

WOMAN SPEAKER Yes, and if the money hadn't been spent on nuclear weapons you would have built up industry.

VOICE FROM CROWD Get back to bloody Russia where you belong.

As the SPEAKER *continues, a Salvation Army band marches down the street, oblivious to all the noise.*

34. Interior. A church. Day.

A packed congregation are praying with their heads bowed. MR AND MRS BECKETT *are among them.*

MINISTER   Let us pray.

The congregation begin the Lord's Prayer. Over an external shot of the church are superimposed the following captions:

'12 noon, U.S. ultimatum expires.
1300. B-52 strike with conventional weapons on Mashad base. Russians defend base with nuclear-tipped air defence missile. Many B-52s lost.
1400. US respond with single battlefield nuclear weapon on Soviet base. Exchange stops'.

35. Documentary footage.

News footage of policemen moving away demonstrators.

36. Interior. Beckett's House. Day.

A news broadcast is going on, while MRS BECKETT *sits and knits baby clothes.*

NEWSREADER   Since the expiry of the deadline at noon yesterday, there have been intense diplomatic efforts to mediate between the two countries.

There is still no information from Iran itself. No news items have been allowed in or out of the country since phone and telex links were cut on Friday evening.

Questioned in the House this morning, the Foreign Secretary said he had no definite news to report and that it would be unhelpful to speculate in the absence of any hard information from the area.

37. Documentary footage.

>*News footage of a man in a street, watching as a convoy of heavy machinery passes. We see aeroplanes, and a long queue at a supermarket checkout. The newsreader's voice continues over this.*

NEWSREADER   There's been a run on tinned food, sugar and other storable items, which is causing shortages in some areas. Spokesmen for the main supermarket chains have said that panic buying is unnecessary.

38. Interior. Local Supermarket. Day.

>*The interior of a small supermarket. The shelves are half empty of goods. The place is crowded and the customers are filling their baskets with what is left. There is an air of tension in the shop. The newsreader's voice continues over this.*

NEWSREADER   Fuel shortages are hindering resupply in some areas but overall there is no shortage of stocks.

>*MR KEMP is one of the customers filling his basket with what is left on the shelves. At the checkout, a woman is arguing with MR HASLAM the shopkeeper.*

WOMAN   40p! That's scandalous. They were only 26p last week.

MR HASLAM   You can always shop somewhere else, you know, if you're not satisfied.

MR KEMP   Honestly! There's a national emergency on and all you can think about is lining your pockets.

MR HASLAM   Look, nobody's forcing you to buy them. Put them back on the shelf if you don't want them.

WOMAN   Yes, I will. I'd sooner starve first. Excuse me.

>*As she goes to put them back, a TEENAGE BOY puts his head round the door. Finding who he's looking for, he calls out.*

BOY   They've started fighting, Mum.

WOMAN   Who has?

BOY	The Americans and the Russians. It's just been on the news. My dad says you've to come home now.
	There is immediate consternation in the shop as everyone starts talking and worrying. The WOMAN *immediately makes for the door, still carrying her basket of goods. Everybody follows her, none of them stopping to pay for their goods.*
MR HASLAM	Hey! You haven't paid for them things.
	But he is too late. Nobody takes any notice of him, and they all rush out of the shop.

39. Exterior. Supermarket. Day.

The customers are emerging from the shop, clutching groceries and stuffing them into their bags, and running in all directions. One woman pushes a loaded trolley down the street. As the street empties, the newsreader's voice comes over the scene.

NEWSREADER In response to today's news of the outbreak of hostilities between vessels of the United States and Soviet Navies, a special session of Parliament has this evening passed an Emergency Powers Act.

40. Exterior. Kemps' garden. Night.

We are in the garden of the Kemps' house. Through the wire of the cage we see JIMMY *in the aviary. On the shelf there is a book, beer and a radio. We hear the radio news.*

NEWSREADER There will be a special announcement at the end of this bulletin, and details will be given of how this affects you. The Prime Minister is expected to address the nation on the international crisis later this evening.

A statement issued earlier from Downing Street said the Government is optimistic that a peaceful negotiated settlement to the conflict is at hand. In the meantime, the public is urged to remain calm and to continue normally.

41. Documentary Footage.

Police cars roar through the streets at night, sirens wailing. People move about in the yellow glow of the street lights. Shouts and screams can be heard near a broken shop window, smashed by someone on the rampage for food. Policemen carry away demonstrators.

42. Interior. Kemps' house. Night.

The Kemps' bedroom. MR AND MRS KEMP *are lying in bed, awake but silent: neither can sleep. Outside there are shouts and screams as people rush about the streets.*

MRS KEMP   You alright, luv?

MR KEMP   It's noisy.

MRS KEMP   Must be pubs turning out.

MR KEMP turns to look at the bedside clock. Its face shows 0040 hours — way past pub closing time. The Kemps lie in silence.

43. Exterior. Kemps' house. Day.

Caption: 'Tuesday May 24th'.

MR KEMP *comes out of the house to collect the milk. He looks tired, after a sleepless night. From indoors we can hear the sound of a radio.*

RADIO INTERVIEWER   ... Nevertheless, people are alarmed at what they see as a lack of advice or information from the Government.

MINISTER   The policy of the Government is quite clear on the matter, we're urging people to keep calm, use their commonsense and go about their business as normal. Panic can only make matters worse. We all know the situation is serious but we are in constant touch with our allies in Washington and have firm assurance that it's under control.

The radio conversation fades down, so that we can hear the conversation between MR KEMP *and his neighbour* MR

STOTHARD. *The Stothards have been packing their car, getting ready to evacuate their house. Elsewhere on the street we see people with suitcases: the normally quiet road is busy with traffic.*

MR KEMP Doing a moonlight flit, then?

MR STOTHARD No. We're going to our Jack's in Lincolnshire while things get sorted out. I reckon we'll be safer over there.

MRS STOTHARD *(to her daughter, who is playing in the doorway)* Carol, will you stop messing about there and come inside the house and do something to help.

MR KEMP It'll not be safe anywhere as far as I can see.

MR STOTHARD I don't know, but there's better chance of surviving out in the country, really haven't we? I mean, where our Jack lives there's only a row of houses and a pub. I don't think they're going to bomb that, are they?

MRS STOTHARD Well, I think that's about it, Ron. Carol.

MR STOTHARD Have you turned that gas off?

MR KEMP I hope so. We don't want the whole street blowing up while you're away.

MR STOTHARD Come on, Carol!

CAROL *(from inside)* Spot, I'm coming. *(She appears at the door).* I can't find our Spot.

MRS STOTHARD Well, he was here a minute ago, wan't he? Have you looked inside the house?

CAROL I've looked upstairs, along the street, next door neighbour's garden, all over.

MRS STOTHARD Honestly, it's ridiculous all this. Spot!

MR STOTHARD Come on. Come on, we're going without him.

CAROL He'll be here in a minute, I know he will be. Spot!

MR STOTHARD Well, we're not standing about here all day waiting for a bloody dog. Get in. Carol, get in.

The family gets in the car, and finally the dog appears and jumps in with them.

Come on. Get in, you bloody thing. See you, then, Bill.

MR KEMP Let's hope so.

MR KEMP *picks up the milk and goes back into the house, shutting the door. As he does so, the sound of the radio—which has been heard very faintly throughout this scene, as the minister and the interviewer discuss the recent mobilisation of British troops—fades up once more.*

RADIO INTERVIEWER Thank you, Minister. And we've just had a newsflash from Bonn that the Russians have cut the road links into and out of West Berlin. Rail and air communications with the city have apparently also been severed. Details are still coming in, but it seems an American convoy, bound for West Berlin, has been turned back at Helmstedt on the East German border. Unconfirmed reports say the Russians have offered safe passage out of the city to the U.S., British and French garrisons. It's not clear yet if this move is connected with yesterday's riots in East Germany. We'll bring you more details on the story as soon as we have them.

44. Interior. Mr Sutton's Office. Later that morning.

MR SUTTON *is working at his desk in his office. The telephone rings and he picks it up. As he speaks, we see the photograph of his wife on the desk.*

MR SUTTON Sutton here... Yes, I understand. Do I have to go right away?... No? When?... Yes, I see...

He puts the receiver down.

45. Various.

JIMMY *is working at the joinery. Hospital ambulances are moving down the roads.*

NEWSREADER Local authorities have been given the power to suspend certain peacetime functions and to requisition premises and materials for civil defence purposes. A government spokesman said that this was a precautionary move only. It was not a cause for alarm.

46. Documentary footage.

Captions over the footage read: 'U.S. Carrier "Kittyhawk" sunk in Persian Gulf'. 'American air and naval blockade of Cuba', 'Anti-Soviet demonstrations in U.S. cities'. 'Damage to Russian Consulates'. 'Further riots in East Germany'.

47. Documentary footage.

A large hospital is being evacuated. Patients are being carried into ambulances on stretchers and wheelchairs.

Superimposed caption: 'Hospitals cleared for expected casualties'.

48. Exterior. Beckett's House. Day.

MR AND MRS BECKETT *are helping* MR BECKETT'S MOTHER *up the steps of the house. She looks frail and ill and moves slowly, for she has just come out of hospital.*

Cut to documentary footage of heavy traffic, people in the streets listening to radios, queues for petrol and 'Closed' signs outside garages with policemen guarding them.

NEWSREADER *(voice-over)* The AA and RAC have reported heavy congestion on roads up and down the country, particularly those leading to Wales and the West Country. The police are urging motorists not to travel unless absolutely necessary and, if it *is* essential, to use only minor roads and leave motorways and inter-city trunk routes clear for official traffic. A full list of designated essential service routes is posted outside your local authority headquarters. It includes the M1, M18, A63 and A629.

49. Exterior. Sheffield. Day.

Caption: 'Emergency powers. (1) Key points guarded. (2) Known and potential subversives arrested'.

We see policemen arresting people and putting them in the back of police transit vans. One of the people arrested is the WOMAN SPEAKER *from the rally. She is pushed into a police car and driven away.*

50. Exterior. Motorway. Day.

There is a huge traffic jam on the motorway. Policemen are speaking to people in cars. One POLICEMAN *is using a loudhailer.*

POLICEMAN *(loudhailer)* This is an Essential Service Route. This is an Essential Service Route. Unless you have official or essential business, please find an alternative route.

We see that the Stothards' car is among the rest. A POLICEMAN *approaches them, and* MR STOTHARD *winds down the window.*

MR STOTHARD We're trying to get across to relatives in Lincolnshire.

POLICEMAN Not this way you're not. Essential services only. You'll have to find another route I'm afraid.

MR STOTHARD Well that's bloody ridiculous. You can't just stop people like that...

Two people are trying to make their way on foot. ANOTHER POLICEMAN *walks over to stop them.*

POLICEMAN Excuse me, where are you going? I'm sorry luv, you can't go up there. You'll have to go back.

Cut back to the Stothards.

POLICEMAN I tell you what...

MR STOTHARD *(interrupting)* You can't just stop people like that.

POLICEMAN I tell you what, try junction 35 or 36 of the M1. They've opened up the hard shoulder for single line traffic only. But you can imagine what it'll be like—it'll be chock-a-block. If I was you I'd go home and sit tight. That's what they're advising people to do.

The POLICEMAN *walks off and* MR STOTHARD *winds up the window of the car.*

POLICEMAN *(loudhailer)* This is an Essential Service Route. This is an Essential Service Route. Unless you have official or essential business, please find an alternative route. This route is for essential traffic only.

51. Interior. Town Hall, Sheffield. Day.

Caption: 'Wednesday May 25th'.

In Mr Sutton's office the television is on, showing the breakfast time news. We see that there is a camp-bed in the room; MR SUTTON *has been sleeping on it.*

NEWSREADER There's growing evidence tonight from scientists and observers in many countries that there have been two nuclear explosions in the Middle East. There's no official confirmation of what has happened and the Foreign Office in London say they have no comment on the report. The evidence all points to two major explosions on...

The voice fades to a faint background noise, analysing the reports from the Middle East.

Meanwhile MRS SUTTON *is packing a suitcase for her husband.* MR SUTTON *is on the telephone, holding on for the person at the other end.*

MRS SUTTON I've put half a dozen in. I can fetch some more if you like.

MR SUTTON No, that'll be plenty. *(Into telephone)* Well, tell him to improvise, then! Right. *(He hangs up.)*

MRS SUTTON Clive, you don't think anything's really going to happen, do you?

MR SUTTON No, it's just a precaution, that's all.

MRS SUTTON Have you had a shave this morning? You should never have said you'd do it. You don't have to. You won't get the sack if you refuse.

MR SUTTON Look, Marjorie. It's difficult for me as well, you know. I don't want to go and leave you and the children.

MRS SUTTON Well then, why are you going?

MR SUTTON Well, somebody's to pick up the pieces if... Look, why didn't you say something before if you were worried about it? You never said anything when I went away on those courses.

The telephone rings, and MR SUTTON *answers it.*

Sutton here... Yes, in about half an hour's time.

He covers the mouthpiece and turns to his wife.

I should be getting off now if I were you. The roads'll be getting busy.

Continuing on telephone.

Use your common sense, man. Well, how should I know?

MRS SUTTON, *upset and worried, is doing up the washbag.*

Marjorie, leave that. I'll ring you later.

Yes... Yes...

MR SUTTON *puts family photographs in his case.*

52. Exterior. Sheffield City Centre. Day.

Documentary footage of policemen all in a line. Then we cut to a rally in the centre of the city, where a TRADE UNIONIST *is speaking to a large crowd.*

TRADE UNIONIST It is imperative while there is still time left that the TUC call a general strike in protest against this disaster which faces us all.

VOICE FROM CROWD That's what destroyed this country!

TRADE UNIONIST There is still time to avert disaster if we act resolutely and show both the Americans and the Russians that we will have no truck with their warmongering.

MAN IN CROWD What about the Falklands?

TRADE UNIONIST	There's nobody more patriotic than me, mate! I've been trying to get us out of the Common Market for bloody years!

The crowd are becoming more noisy and restless. As the police move further in to try and disperse the rally, scuffles break out and things get more chaotic.

TRADE UNIONIST	Please, do not play into their hands. This is a peaceful demonstration. We are exercising our right of free speech. The police have no right to stop this demonstration.

Amidst the chaos we catch sight of a street trader selling tin openers.

TRADER	Tin openers! £1.50 a go. Come on, all of you, £1.50. It could save your life.

53. Interior. Art Gallery. Day.

Two attendants are taking down pictures from the walls of the city art gallery and are carefully loading them onto a trolley. We see a Lowry painting. The riot noise can be heard from outside, and we cut to documentary footage of the riots.

54. Interior. Control Room. Day.

A dimly lit corridor. MR SUTTON *comes downstairs into the control room. The* CHIEF SUPERINTENDENT *comes to meet him.*

MR SUTTON	Morning, Alan.
CHIEF SUPERINTNDT	Morning, Clive.
MR SUTTON	What's it like in there?
CHIEF SUPERINTNDT	Oh, a bit primitive—take a look.
MR SUTTON	Ah well, we'll get it organized.

Carries on walking. STEVE, *a young man with a clipboard, stands in the doorway. Inside the control room there are people busy doing jobs, setting up various machines and so on.*

Where the hell is everybody? There's only half of them here.

CHIEF SUPERINTNDT You know Steve, the Information Officer?

MR SUTTON Where the hell is everybody?

STEVE Geoff just rang in to say his car's broken down...

MR SUTTON Well, that's no good, is it? How many are we missing?

STEVE Ten.

MR SUTTON Well, get on the phone and tell them I want them here immediately.

STEVE Right.

MR SUTTON Which is my desk?

CHIEF SUPERINTNDT It's straight through. Mind your head.

MR SUTTON I don't see any sign of the Emergency Committee, do you?

CHIEF SUPERINTNDT You know what bloody councillors are like.

MR SUTTON They're not getting paid for this lot, are they?

CHIEF SUPERINTNDT Well, this is it. Best I could do.

He walks away. A man with a clipboard comes up to MR SUTTON *and shakes hands with him.*

MEDICAL OFFICER Dr Carlton. Regional Health Authority.

MR SUTTON How do you do? How's thing going?

MEDICAL OFFICER We're doing our best.

MR SUTTON Good.

COMMENTARY *(voice-over)*. In the last few days. Emergency Headquarters like this one have been hastily improvised up and down the country in the basements of town halls and civic centres.

We see everyone trying to settle into the Emergency Headquarters. Bunk beds are being set up in one room, and a man brings in a portable loo.

55. Interior. The empty flat. Night.

Documentary footage: planes taking off.

JIMMY *and* RUTH *are stripping the walls of the bedroom in their new flat. A transistor radio is broadcasting the Protect and Survive information.* RUTH *is deeply upset by what she is hearing.*

BROADCASTER The time has now come to make everything ready for you and your family in case an air attack happens. This does not mean war is bound to come, but there is a risk of this and we must all be prepared.

Sound of siren warning.

When you hear the attack warning you and your family must take cover at once. Do not stay out of doors. If you are caught in the open, lie down.

JIMMY *is working, oblivious of* RUTH.

JIMMY Will you pass us that er...

He turns and sees RUTH *is crying. He goes to her, takes her in his arms and tries to comfort her.*

BROADCASTER If you leave your home your Local Authority might take it over for homeless families and if you move the authorities in the new place will not help you with food, accommodation or other essentials. You are better off in your own home. Stay there.

We cut to an external shot of their block of flats, with just their light on.

56. Exterior. Sheffield. Night.

Caption: '10.30 p.m. Fire Engines deployed to safety'.

A line of fire engines all leave the station and drive off, with lights flashing but no sirens. A small boy watches, fascinated, from a doorway as the fire engines go down the street and round the corner, and the doors of the fire station close.

57. Exterior. Kemps' street. Day.

Caption: 'Thursday May 26th, 08.00'.

Day is starting in the Kemps' street. A MILKMAN *is beginning his round, delivering to various houses. Over this we hear a public information broadcast.*

BROADCASTER If anyone dies while you are kept in your fallout room, move the body to another room in the house. Label the body with name and address and cover it as tightly as possible in polythene paper, sheets or blankets. If, however, you have had a body in the house for more than five days and if it is safe to go outside, then you should bury the body for the time being in a trench or cover it with earth and mark the spot of the burial.

Alison comes out of the newsagent's, reading a comic. She takes her bicycle and wheels it away.

58. Interior. Becketts' house. Day.

In the bathroom, RUTH *is being sick. The public information broadcast continues from the previous scene.*

BROADCASTER Here are some ideas for making your inner refuge. One. Make a 'lean-to' with sloping doors or strong boards rested against an inner wall. Prevent them from slipping by fixing a length of wood along the floor. Build further protection of bags or boxes of earth or sand, or books, or even clothing, on the slope of your refuge, and anchor these also against slipping. Partly close...

The broadcast continues behind the scene.

Meanwhile RUTH *has come downstairs. She enters the kitchen, where* MR BECKETT *is studying his paper, which has Protect and Survive information printed in it.* MRS BECKETT *is preparing breakfast.*

MRS BECKETT   Are you alright, love?

RUTH   I've just been sick again. I feel awful. I think I'll go back to bed.

MRS BECKETT   Don't worry about it. It'll only last for a week or two. I'd better ring work for you and tell them you're not coming in.

RUTH   If there's anybody there. There were only one or two in yesterday.

MRS BECKETT *is trying to telephone.*

MRS BECKETT   It's worse than before. I can't get anything now. The line's dead.

MR BECKETT   I think we ought to be getting the rest of the things down the cellar now.

Caption: 'Emergency Powers: Non-essential phones disconnected'.

59. Interior. Bunker.

People are trying to organize themselves in the bunker. Some study papers, others are on the telephone. Maps and charts are now on the walls and Protect and Survive information is being broadcast on the television. A speaker, which emits a continual tone, is being labelled 'Attack Warning'. The CHIEF SUPERINTENDENT *and the* INFORMATION OFFICER *are amongst those on the telephone.*

CHIEF SUPERINTNDT   Hello, County. This is Sheffield District. Testing, 1, 2, 3, 4. Please report my signal. Over.

INFORMATION OFFICER   ... well whose bloody responsibility is it, then? ... Look, we've all got families... Look, just get down here, there's nine other people...

CHIEF SUPERINTNDT   Look, I've got a serious public order problem. I need at least an extra six PSUs... Yeah but when?... Look, I'm using traffic wardens already... Alright, then I'll have to swear in some special constables.

COMMENTARY Many of these officers have had no training at all. Some have learned of their emergency role only in the last few days—and almost all are unsure of their exact duties.

60. Interior. Kemps' house. Day.

MRS KEMP is going to and from the kitchen, trying to clear the breakfast table, while MR KEMP is unhinging a door to make a shelter. ALISON is worried about getting to school and MICHAEL is wandering about reading. In the living room the television is on, broadcasting Protect and Survive information on how to build an 'inner refuge'. An air of chaos and confusion hangs over the household.

MR KEMP I suppose I ought to take this one off as well.

MRS KEMP You what! It'll get scratched to bits, and it's only just been painted, Bill.

MR KEMP It's better than getting blown to pieces, isn't it?

ALISON Have I to go to school, then, Mum? I'm going to be late.

MRS KEMP I don't know. What did it say on the telly? I can't remember whether it said the schools were closed or not.

MICHAEL Oh, they're closed. It said so on the news. We've to stay at home.

ALISON Are you sure?

MICHAEL 'Course I am. It said they were sending notes out to all the parents...

MR KEMP Bloody hell, this is tight.

ALISON Great! We had a history test this morning.

MRS KEMP *(shouting from the kitchen)* Alison, run down to Kirby's and see if they've got any food left.

ALISON Like what?

MRS KEMP   Anything. Bread, tinned stuff. Bring whatever you can and take my purse.

MICHAEL   Dad, are you going to build one of these in here?

MRS KEMP   Over my dead body he is. I want to know something more definite before we start ripping this place to pieces.

MICHAEL   Can I help you? It'll be great. I'll be able to sleep in it. It'll be like going camping.

61. Exterior. Sheffield. Day.

A television screen is showing an information film on fallout.

TELEVISION SOUNDTRACK   The most widespread danger is fallout. Fallout is dust that is sucked up from the ground after an explosion. Fallout can kill...

We discover that the television screen is in a shop window. A crowd of people are staring at it. All the other television sets in the shop window are showing the same programme.

In Sheffield town centre, people are queuing outside banks and cash points.

COMMENTARY   *(voice over).* It's 8.30 a.m.—3.30 in the morning in Washington. Over the past four days, neither the President nor his senior staff will have had more than a few hours rest.

This is when they may be asleep. This is when western responses will be slowest.

62. Interior. Bunker.

The FOOD OFFICER *is briefing the other officers in the bunker.*

FOOD OFFICER As we expected, nearly all the supermarket shelves are empty but we've managed to get the warehouses controlled by the police. As yet we haven't located all the root vegetable clumps on local farms but stocks of sugar, wheat, flour and rice are quite good...

Suddenly the Attack Warning alarm begins to give short, sharp bursts of tone.

WOMAN That's it.

VOICE FROM SPEAKER Attack warning red. Attack warning red. *(This is repeated.)*

MALE OFFICER Attack warning. Is it for real?

ANOTHER OFFICER Attack warning. It's for bloody real!

MR SUTTON Right, get to your stations... Get that generator going... and shut the doors.

There is a lot of action, confusion and slight panic in the bunker. We hear the Chief Superintendent on the radio.

CHIEF SUPERINTNDT ... well get your heads down!

63. Exterior. Joinery. Day.

In the joinery yard, BOB *is on the lorry and* JIMMY *standing at the side. A group of men are clustered round them, demanding wood.*

JIMMY Look, we can't sell you any timber. You'll have to see bosses about it... it's a bloody joinery, not a timber yard.

A siren sounds. The group of men stand for a moment, not knowing what to do. JIMMY *reacts first, pulling* BOB *down from the lorry, scattering the men.*

JIMMY Come on! Quick, get down.

They both get underneath the lorry.

64. Various shots of Sheffield. Day.

People are screaming and running in all directions, not knowing what to do. A police car moves down a street, its siren going.

Caption: '08.35: single warhead explodes high above

North Sea. Energy pulse burns out many electrical systems'.

Power lines arc and flash and a domestic iron blows up. We cut back to JIMMY *and* BOB *under the lorry with their hands over their heads.*

Caption: 'Massive damage to communications across Britain and North West Europe'.

A transistor blows up and a computer in the bunker goes dead. Someone starts trying to make it work.

MAN IN BUNKER: These are gone. Everything's dead. Why didn't you pull the bloody aerial out?... Move that, come on!

65. Documentary footage.

Deserted gatehouses at RAF Finningley. A plane takes off.

Caption: '08.37. First missile salvo hits NATO military targets'.

Cut to the planes. Another siren is sounding, and a mushroom cloud goes up in the sky.

66. Montage sequence.

A great flash occurs and we see people in the city centre dazzled by the light. Their faces are screwed up and they try to shield their eyes with their hands. A car skids off the road and into a wall.

In the Kemps' house, MR KEMP *is on the toilet.*

MR KEMP: Bloody hell!

He hurriedly pulls up his trousers.

In the Becketts' house, MR AND MRS BECKETT *are helping* GRANNY BECKETT *down the stairs.*

GRANNY: Hold on, Gordon, you're going too fast.

The mushroom cloud again; faces appear with disbelief and

terror on them. A woman wets herself. The blast wave arrives, creating smoke and flying debris. The screams get worse.

JIMMY and BOB are still lying under the lorry surrounded by dust and a rushing wind.

In the Kemps' house MRS KEMP is holding MICHAEL tightly to her, to try and shield him from the blast.

In the Becketts' house MR AND MRS BECKETT are helping the old lady down the stairs of the cellar.

67. Exterior. Joinery. Day.

JIMMY and BOB are flat on their faces under the lorry. All around them there is screaming, windows smashing and dogs barking. JIMMY raises his head.

JIMMY   Come on, that'll only be the start of it.

He scrambles out from under the lorry, pulling BOB with him. As they stand they look to the sky and see the mushroom clouds rising above Sheffield. BOB stares in sheer disbelief.

BOB   Jesus Christ! They've done it. They've done it.

JIMMY runs off.

BOB   Where are you going?

JIMMY   *(getting into his car)* I'm going to try to get to Ruth. See if she's alright.

He tries to start it but without success.

Come on!... Oh shit!

He gets out and runs off, leaving BOB still standing, rooted to the spot. We follow JIMMY, running through the smoky streets, past panic-stricken people and scenes of devastation. JIMMY is impervious to it all.

68. Interior. Kemps' house. Day.

There is frantic activity as MR AND MRS KEMP try to build

a shelter in the room. They have a door against the wall and various blankets and bundles of clothes lying about the place. MR KEMP *is carrying a mattress.*

MR KEMP No, that's wrong—get all that stuff off. We've got to get the mattress on the bottom. That's right. Put it there. Right, build it up.

Starts to frantically put clothes and blankets over the shelter.

MRS KEMP *(crying)* JIMMY *and* ALISON...

MR KEMP Build it up!

69. Interior. The bunker control room. Day.

Some officers and others are crowded around the map and chart on the wall. Everyone is talking, on radios and telephones, or to each other. Everyone is frightened. We hear snatches of conversation, relating mainly to the map and chart.

TRANSPORT OFFICER What's that?... There's nothing there... Is it a power station?

FOOD OFFICER No, that's up at Ferrybridge.

SCIENTIFIC ADVISOR According to County they've hit Finningley... Bawtry...

ACCOMMODTN OFFICER What about Doncaster... 5803... where's 58...?

WORKS OFFICER They're bound to have copped it, aren't they? It's just up the road from Finningley.

SCIENTIFIC ADVISOR There's something on the airport, I think.

Caption: 'Eighty megatons fall on UK'.

70. Montage sequence.

The mushroom cloud. People in pain and rushing about. JIMMY *is still running along the street.*

Caption: 'Blast casualties between two-and-a-half and nine million'.

In the Becketts' house they are still on the cellar steps. MRS BECKETT *is shining a torch.*

MR BECKETT Shine the torch further down, love. Ruth!

RUTH *is standing at the top of the cellar steps, doing nothing.*

MR BECKETT Come down here and give us a hand. Ruth! Come and help with your grandmother.

RUTH *slips out of the house. We see* JIMMY *running in the streets.*

Caption: 'Communications in chaos'.

Inside the Kemps' house they are still trying to build the shelter. MRS KEMP *is crying.*

Caption: 'Command and control links failing'.

Outside in the street, people are running around. Among them is RUTH, *running away from the house. She collides with someone, enabling* MR BECKETT *to catch up with her. Protesting, she allows him to take her back to the house.*

The mushroom cloud again.

Caption: 'Nuclear exchanges escalate'.

JIMMY *is running through the streets, trying to get to Ruth's house. By now he is looking tired.*

A series of images of Sheffield come on screen, showing steelworks and power stations.

Caption: 'Priority economic targets: Energy, Steel, Chemicals'.

In the Kemps' back garden MICHAEL *is sitting in the ruins of the aviary, crying. Some of the birds are dead. Inside the house,* MRS KEMP *suddenly realizes* MICHAEL *is not with them. She calls his name.*

As she does so the screen goes white as a one-megaton bomb airbursts over the Sheffield/Rotherham industrial area.

A series of effects: a toy model of E.T. melts; milk bottles on the doorstep boil and explode; Mrs Kemp's clothes and the curtains are on fire. Then the blast wave hits the house: the window bursts inwards and everything is obscured as debris rains down and objects fly in all directions.

71. Exterior. Sheffield. Day.

A series of images of Sheffield after the blast has hit: the smoke of the mushroom cloud rises. Houses, flats and shops blow up—among them 'Woolworths' and 'British Home Stores'. Buildings collapse.

72. Interior. Bunker control room.

As the blast hits, the bunker shudders and plaster and debris fall down. A large beam falls, hitting someone on the head. Screams ring out and the lights fail.

Caption: 'East-West exchange three thousand megatons. Two hundred and ten megatons fall on UK'.

Caption: 'Two-thirds of houses in Britain within possible fire zones'.

73. Exterior. Sheffield. Day.

After the blast. We see the details of the burning ruins of Sheffield: liquid gushes from pipes; a milk float burns; a figure crawls through the ruins; a teddy bear is on fire; a bus is on its side, burning amongst other vehicles. A bicycle is wedged in a tree on fire. An injured cat staggers and falls dead; a charred hand reaches from the rubble; blood gushes out from the bricks; charred and burning corpses lie among the devastation.

74. Interior. Bunker.

Caption: 'Fallout imminent. Firefighting and rescue attempts unlikely'.

Chaos reigns in the bunker, which is initially lit by a couple of candles. The generator is turned on, revealing dust, plaster and debris everywhere. Everybody is trying to get organised—attempting, without much success—to use the radios and telephones.

MR SUTTON Well done, Gordon. How long can you keep that going?

VOICE We've diesel for two weeks if we're careful.

A man has been hurt by a fallen beam. The CHIEF SUPERINTENDENT *and the* MEDICAL OFFICER *kneel to tend to him.*

CHIEF SUPERINTNDT First aid kit, quickly!

INFORMATION OFFICER We've lost County again, I think. Aerials must have blown. They're on the roof.

MR SUTTON Can you raise any of the districts?... Well, what about the radio hams? Can we improvise an aerial?

OFFICER Well, we'll try.

The MEDICAL OFFICER *is still tending the wounded man.*

VOICE Where the hell's the first aid kit?

VOICE It's on the shelf at the back.

SHOUT FROM THE BACK It's all blocked out here. I can't shift a thing.

CHIEF SUPERINTNDT How is he?

MEDICAL OFFICER He's dead.

SHOUT FROM THE BACK I can't find this first aid kit.

MEDICAL OFFICER Forget the first aid kit. Bring me something to cover him up with.

75. Exterior. Sheffield. Day.

The city is burning.

76. Interior. Kemps' house.

In a very smoky living room MR AND MRS KEMP *are huddled in their makeshift shelter, which has been badly damaged.* MRS KEMP *keeps murmuring* MICHAEL's *name.* MR KEMP *coughs badly and dabs at* MRS KEMP's *burns, which are severe. She cries out from the agonizing pain.*

77. Interior. The Becketts' cellar.

The cellar is in darkness.

MR BECKETT. Everybody alright?

No reply.

Mother?

MR BECKETT *shines his torch about, revealing* RUTH *crying and huddled in a corner, then* MRS BECKETT, *who is coughing and trying to mend her glasses, which have been smashed in the chaos.* MR BECKETT *takes her hand in comfort. Suddenly the cellar is struck by another tremor. There are screams and plaster and bricks fall.*

MRS BECKETT Isn't it ever going to stop?

78. Interior. Bunker.

In the bunker they are experiencing the same tremor as the Becketts.

SOMEONE Jesus Christ. Not another one.

Static bursts on the radio.

SOMEONE It's the Stocksbridge police.

The CHIEF SUPERINTENDENT *is trying to carry on a conversation with someone on the radio, but the connection is very poor.*

CHIEF SUPERINTNDT What about rescue? Is there anything you can do? Over.

Meanwhile, the MEDICAL OFFICER *and* ANOTHER MAN *are putting a dead body into bin liners.*

MEDICAL OFFICER	Get me another bin liner.
CHIEF SUPERINTNDT	What's your radiac reading? I repeat—what's your radiac reading? Over... A hundred... It's too high. You've got to get your men under cover. Can you... could you... can you get us through to County Central Headquarters?... Over. Can you patch us through, over? Stocksbridge, are you receiving me, over?... We've lost them.

At another radio set, the INFORMATION OFFICER *is having a conversation which can just be heard.*

INFORMATION OFFICER	What about Division Street and Elm Lane? Have you heard anything from there?
RADIO VOICE	Not a thing. They'll be totally wiped out. I should think, judging by what it's like here.
VOICE	Hey! We've got a fire station.
REPLY	Where?
VOICE	High Green, I think. We've got a D.F.O. coming through!

Other officers are trying to get the INFORMATION OFFICER *to ask questions.*

INFORMATION OFFICER	What about Hillsborough and Stocksbridge?
RADIO VOICE	Nothing from Hillsborough, but Stocksbridge not too bad... Windows blown in and structural damage, but not too bad.
INFORMATION OFFICER	Windows blown in that far out. Jesus Christ!
MANPOWER OFFICER	Ask him where that last one was! Ask him where that last one was!

MR SUTTON *is sitting in his chair, looking up at the air vent, which is billowing out dust.*

MR SUTTON	Switch that thing off will you, Gordon?

79. Various shots of fallout.

The fallout plume. Dust settles on broken windows and doors.

COMMENTARY   The first fallout dust settles on Sheffield. It's an hour and twenty-five minutes after the attack. An explosion on the ground at Crewe has sucked up this debris and made it radioactive. The wind has blown it here.

This level of attack has broken most of the windows in Britain. Many roofs are open to the sky. Some of the lethal dust gets in.

In these early stages, the symptoms of radiation sickness and the symptoms of panic are identical.

Inside the Kemps' shelter, MR KEMP *is being violently sick into his handkerchief.*

80. Interior. Becketts' cellar.

In the dimly-lit cellar, MR BECKETT *is at the lavatory bucket being sick.* MRS BECKETT *is tending to* GRANNY. RUTH *is huddled in a blanket, drinking out of a bottle.*

MR BECKETT   Are you alright, Ruth? Ruth?

RUTH   What?

MR BECKETT   Are you feeling alright?

GRANNY   I couldn't help it. It just came on...

MRS BECKETT   Don't worry about it, love. It's not your fault. We've all got it. It's the shock.

GRANNY   I know, but I feel so ashamed...

MRS BECKETT   It's the shock. It's the shock, isn't it, Gordon? Come on, lie down.

GRANNY   Messing the bed at my age. It's like being a little baby again.

MRS BECKETT   Ruth, come and help me to clean grandma up.

RUTH makes no attempt to move, but carries on drinking.

MRS BECKETT Ruth, be careful with that, lovey, you don't know how long it's going to have to last us.

MR BECKETT Go on, Ruth, don't just sit there. Do something for once.

We hear MR BECKETT *being sick again.* RUTH *gets up and goes to help her mother, but as soon as the blankets are drawn back she retches violently and turns away. The sight and the smell are too much for her.*

81. Interior. Kemps' house.

Caption: 'Friday May 27th. Attack plus one day'.

Inside the shelter we hear MRS KEMP *whimpering in great pain: her burns have turned septic.*

MRS KEMP Michael. Michael. I've got to find him.

MR KEMP You, you stop here and I'll go and look for him.

MRS KEMP No, no. I want to come. I want to go as well.

MR KEMP You stop here, luv. I'll only be out a few minutes. No need to look. Stop here, luv.

MRS KEMP I've got to come. Help me.

The both struggle from their shelter. Outside they are confronted by a scene of complete devastation.

MR KEMP Oh my god! Michael... Michael!

Frantically, they search for their son, scrabbling at the rubble. They do not have long to search before they see MICHAEL's *foot sticking out from under the debris.*

82. Interior. Bunker.

Caption: 'Sunday May 29th. Attack plus three days'.

We see the ventilator. Nearby a man is lying collapsed on the floor. There is a lot of noise and general hubbub. Someone is trying to communicate on the radio.

VOICE	... for two days... Well, who the hell else have you tried?... Well, send another motorcycle.
ANOTHER VOICE	There are no roads left.

The SCIENTIFIC ADVISOR *and* MR SUTTON *are looking over a map. On* MR SUTTON's *desk is a photograph of his wife.*

SCIENTIFIC ADVISOR	All the people here will be dead already. It's completely flattened round here. About 50% will still be alive but here they're as good as dead already. They've probably received a lethal dose.
MR SUTTON	What about here?

He is pointing to the village where he lived.

SCIENTIFIC ADVISOR	It'll be really heavy there. If the wind's still blowing from the West South West, it's in a direct line from Crewe. Eight hundred rads? A thousand? Difficult to say. Depends on what sort of cover they've got. Of course, if they've got a decent cellar...

Around them, lots of people are shouting and arguing about a variety of subjects.

OFFICER	You're wanted on the radio.
WORKS OFFICER	There's no way of getting anything out. According to the re...
OFFICER ON RADIO	Yeah, Yes. I'll pass the message on.
WORKS OFFICER	What am I expected to do?
TRANSPORT OFFICER	What about Knutton Road and Grenoside? What's it like there?

The man from the radio comes up with a message on a piece of paper.

MAN FROM RADIO	Hey, listen. I've got a message from Rivelin Valley police, they've managed to get through to Beauchief Works

	Dept. They've got some vehicles on the road but they're nearly out of fuel.
WORKS OFFICER	Well, what the bloody hell have they been doing with it?
MAN FROM RADIO	They didn't tell me. They just said they want to know if they can get some more and they've got no food.
MANPOWER OFFICER	Any chance of getting through to County?
MEDICAL OFFICER	Look, I've got. . .
WORKS OFFICER	Just let me get on with it. O.K.?

83. Exterior. Food warehouse. Day.

Caption: 'Attack plus one week. Food stores controlled by central government representatives'.

Outside a food warehouse a soldier is standing guard. Another is measuring the radiation with a radiac meter.

Caption: 'No food distribution likely until two weeks after attack'.

84. Interior. Becketts' cellar.

Shot of a filthy lavatory bucket. Cut from that to where MR AND MRS BECKETT *are preparing a meal out of a can.* MR BECKETT *puts a small amount on a plate for Granny.*

MR BECKETT Here you are, mother, something to eat for you. . . Better leave her. The rest will do her good.

No reply from GRANNY.

MRS BECKETT Well, at least it won't go cold. Ruth? Ruth, love.

She offers RUTH *the food.*

RUTH (*sobbing and crying*). No.

MRS BECKETT Come on, love. You'll have to eat something.

Ruth shakes her head.

MRS BECKETT But you'll have to, love. It's not just for you now, you know. The baby needs some food as well. Come on.

RUTH I don't care about this baby any more. I wish it was dead.

MRS BECKETT Oh, Ruth. Don't say things like that.

RUTH There's no point! There's no point with Jimmy dead.

MRS BECKETT You don't know Jimmy's dead, love.

RUTH He is! I know he is!

MRS BECKETT But you can't be certain.

RUTH We're breathing in all this radiation. All the time my baby.

She turns away in tears.

MRS BECKETT What do you mean?

RUTH It'll be deformed.

Cut away to exterior shot of ruins.

85. Interior. The Kemps' shelter.

In the shelter MR KEMP *is being sick into a handkerchief;* MRS KEMP *is delirious.*

MRS KEMP Michael, Michael. Jimmy and Alison... all dead... all three dead.

MR KEMP Oh no, we don't know that. They might be safe somewhere.

MRS KEMP I wish it were me... I wish I were dead.

MR KEMP *(bursting into tears)* I wish I were dead.

86. Interior. The bunker.

Two officers are trying to clear rubble from the entrance. The MEDICAL OFFICER *is giving a man a drink. Everyone is dirty, the men unshaven. Various discussions and arguments are going on.*

VOICE Watch that bloody water.

VOICE How far does this go back?

VOICE There's four floors come down on this lot. It could go back for yards and yards.

There are problems with the ventilator.

VOICE Try it again, Gordon.

VOICE Still nothing coming through. It must be blocked further up.

The CHIEF SUPERINTENDENT *is on the radio.*

CHIEF SUPERINTNDT Well, when will you be able to get to us?

RADIO VOICE We can't get lifting gear through.

CHIEF SUPERINTNDT What about the army? What about military help?

RADIO VOICE Listen, it's chaos out here... mob rule... they're up to their necks as it is.

A few officers are sitting around the main desk.

MR SUTTON We've not heard from County yet.

FOOD OFFICER If we don't release some food soon, we'll never get things under control.

INFORMATION OFFICER You try getting through to them. It's bloody hopeless.

FOOD OFFICER I've got starving mobs in Sharrow, Ecclesfield, Dronfield, Manor Estate...

MR SUTTON Look, it's not our decision, anyway. It's up to Zone to authorise the release of buffer stocks and then it becomes a County decision.

MANPOWER OFFICER We can't get through to County!

FOOD OFFICER So what are we going to do, then? Let them starve?

MR SUTTON	Look, even if we did have the authority...
MANPOWER OFFICER	Look, we're on our own. You've got the authority. It's about bloody time you did something with it.
MR SUTTON	Look, what's the point of wasting food on people who are going to die anyway?
MEDICAL OFFICER	I agree with Clive. The food stocks aren't going to last long. A lot of people just didn't stock up...
FOOD OFFICER	How could they? The bloody shops were empty!
MEDICAL OFFICER	And now they're coming out of their shelters. I know it sounds callous but I think we should hang on to the little food we've got.
MANPOWER OFFICER	And I need that food to force people to work.
FOOD OFFICER	Go and make us a cup of tea, Sharon.
MANPOWER OFFICER	Go and make one yourself. I'm not your bloody wife, you know.
FOOD OFFICER	Anybody got a fag?
MEDICAL OFFICER	*(A poor attempt at a joke)* Bad for your health, you know.

Under this dialogue a radio voice can be heard.

RADIO VOICE	For God's sake send us some reinforcements... it's completely out of control down 'ere... There's about two thousand of 'em outside Mosborough Fire Station... They're trying to get at the food... I've got ten men holding 'em off, but got to pull 'em back... They've had 200 rads as it is. You've got to send some more men. They're pulling the place apart.
CHIEF SUPERINTNDT	*(on the radio)* Look, I don't care how much trouble they're causing. We're not sending our men in there with radiation as high as that.
RADIO VOICE	But we can't hold them back...
CHIEF SUPERINTNDT	Look, I know that, but what's the point? They're gonna die on that patch anyway.

87. Interior. The Kemps' shelter.

MRS KEMP Bill... Bill. Just get me... just get me a drink. Please, a drink...

MR KEMP I'll go and see if I can find anything. I won't be long, love.

He crawls out of the shelter while MRS KEMP *is violently sick.* MR KEMP *stumbles into the wrecked kitchen, goes to the sink and turns on the tap. A dribble of water comes out, but he has no container for it. Searching, he finds a colander, but by the time he has pushed it under the tap, the water has stopped. He lays his head on the sink and coughs badly.*

88. Interior. Becketts' house.

MR BECKETT *struggles through the cellar door, carrying the body of his mother by the shoulders.* RUTH *comes up out of the cellar and stands and watches him.*

MR BECKETT Just a minute. Just a minute.

MRS BECKETT Can you manage?

MR BECKETT Put her down in a minute. Put her down here. Give us those blankets.

He covers the body.

Quietly, RUTH *slips away from the house.*

MR BECKETT Come on. Oh my God!

MRS BECKETT Ruth!

MR BECKETT Ruth!

He goes to his wife and comforts her.

MR BECKETT Come on. Down you go.

They go back to the cellar, MRS BECKETT *sobbing, leaving behind the body of the old woman, completely covered by the blankets apart from her slippered feet sticking out from the bottom.*

89. Exterior. Sheffield. Day.

Caption: 'Sunday June 5th. Attack plus ten days'.

We see the ruins of Sheffield. MR KEMP *is wandering among them, carrying a container, looking for water. Seeing a small trickle he drinks thirstily, then immediately retches. It is contaminated. While this goes on a voice is heard, very faintly.*

VOICE　Radiation levels are still dangerous. Residents of Release Band A—that is Woodseats, Dore and Totley and Abbeydale—should not stay out of their shelters for more than two hours per day. Residents of Release Band B—that is Nether Edge, Banner Cross and Broomhill—no longer than one hour per day.

90. Exterior. Sheffield. Day.

RUTH *is looking for* JIMMY *in the streets. It is dark, cold and smoky, and she wanders through the ruins, numbed, her face showing no emotion. We see the enormity of the devastation of the city with a sinister nightmare quality as various characters and images appear to her.*

A DEMENTED WOMAN *approaches.*

WOMAN　Mandy, have you seen our Mandy?

A man tries to open a sealed packet of ham with his teeth. Two dead bodies lie charred in a car. A SMALL BOY *comes up.*

BOY　Mum? Mum?

A MAN *lays out toy figures on a stone. Charred remains of dead bodies lie in the ruins—hands, faces and legs. A* LITTLE OLD LADY *sits huddles in a blanket. A* MAN *shakes violently with a bandaged face, and a* WOMAN *suckles a dead baby in her arms.*

91. Interior. The Becketts' Cellar.

Amid the gloom of the cellar MR AND MRS BECKETT *are sitting huddled together in blankets, depressed.*

MRS BECKETT   What time is it?

MR BECKETT   Half past two.

MRS BECKETT   Night... night or day?

MR BECKETT   Night, I think. I'm not sure. I'm losing track. I'm not sure whether it's night or day anymore.

Noises are heard from upstairs. We see a pair of feet prowling over the floor. The BECKETTS *are terrified. The footsteps fade and we see the dead body once more.*

92. The atmosphere.

Shots of dramatic skies.

Caption: 'Three thousand megaton exchange. Smoke produced: one hundred million tons. Dust lifted into atmosphere: five hundred million tons'.

COMMENTARY   Hanging in the atmosphere, the clouds of debris shut out the sun's heat and light. Across large areas of the northern hemisphere it starts to get dark. It starts to get cold.

Shots of refugees and wounded people, huddled together.

COMMENTARY   In the centres of large land masses like America or Russia, the temperature drop may be severe, as much as 25 degrees centigrade. Even in Britain—within days of the attack—it could fall to freezing or below for long dark periods.

93. Interior. Kemps' house. Day.

Caption: 'Monday June 6th. Attack plus The Kemps' house is devastated. Inside, MRS KEMP *is lying alone, dead.* RUTH *stands in the doorway, looking down at the body, not shocked by what she sees. She picks up a book on birds, and leaves the house.*

94. Exterior. Food Warehouse. Day.

A scene of violence and confusion. A large and angry mob of people—among them MR KEMP—*are gathered at the gates of the warehouse, hungry and in desperate need of food. Behind the gates, guarding the warehouse are an officer and some soldiers, holding their weapons at the ready.* THE OFFICER *speaks through his megaphone, trying to calm the crowd, but he only makes them more angry.*

OFFICER Go back to yor homes. The allocation of food stores will begin shortly. The distribution points will be announced.

VOICES IN CROWD We want it now! We're starving!

OFFICER I repeat. Go home. There is nothing we can do. We have no authority to distribute food.

VOICES IN CROWD Who are you saving it for?

The fence is being shaken violently. It looks as if it will not hold.

OFFICER This is a warning. Any attempt to appropriate provisions from these premises will be met by force. So I advise you again to disperse and go back to your homes. . .

A man is climbing the gate. At an order from the officer, the soldiers pull down their gas masks.

OFFICER Prepare to fire gas. One round. C.S. Gas, base of gate. One round at that man.

The people scatter in the smoke.

95. Exterior. Lodge Moor Hospital. Day.

Caption: 'Saturday June 11th. Attack plus sixteen days'.

Hundreds of people are trying to get up the steps of the hospital; they have all kinds of injuries. In the crowd is RUTH, *continually looking at faces to see if* JIMMY *is among them.*

Inside the building there are scenes of indescribable squalor. The place is overrun with people, sitting on every space on the floor, up the steps, in the corridor, everywhere. Nurses are ripping cloth for bandages; auxiliaries are hurrying about exhausted. Sacks of salt are being poured into water. All around are horrifying screams, caused by operations being carried on without anaesthetic. We see a doctor sawing at a leg to amputate it.

COMMENTARY The entire peacetime resources of the British Health Service—even if they survived—would be unable to cope with the effects of even the single bomb that's hit Sheffield.

By this time, without drugs, water or bandages, without electricity or medical support facilities, there is virtually no way a doctor can exercise his skill. As a source of help or comfort he's little better equipped than the nearest survivor.

RUTH *walks among the people and up the stairs, which are dripping with a foul-coloured liquid.*

96. Interior. Bunker.

Only a few of the officers are left with the strength to carry on. Their tempers are frayed and most of them have come to the end of their tethers. The room is candlelit and the air is stale and murky. The table is covered with food, empty cigarette packets and coffee cups.

MR SUTTON We've no choice as far as I can see.

FOOD OFFICER Can't we get any food from outside?

MR SUTTON Where from? We've talked to County and everybody's in the same boat, aren't they?

OFFICER What about the broiler fowls that've died? Can't we use them? They'll just rot if we don't. Problem is, we can't contact Rockley and Haresbrook. God knows what's happened there.

FOOD OFFICER Probably been raided...

MR SUTTON	What do you think, Doctor?
MEDICAL OFFICER	We'll have to cut their rations. I've worked it out here. One thousand calories for manual workers and five hundred for the rest.
FOOD OFFICER	Five hundred! Five hundred! That wouldn't keep a flea alive!
MR SUTTON	Should we be bothering to keep anybody alive if they can't work?
MEDICAL OFFICER	A lot of people are going to die anyway. It's back to survival of the fittest, I suppose.
MR SUTTON	What's that in terms of food then, five hundred calories?
MEDICAL OFFICER	I don't know. A few slices of bread. Some soup. A lamb chop. Treacle tart. A few pints of beer.

He pauses and shakes his fist in anger and looks towards the 'sky'.

MEDICAL OFFICER	Bastards!

The CHIEF SUPERINTENDENT *and the* ACCOMMODATION OFFICER *are in heated argument about what to do with detainees.*

CHIEF SUPERINTNDT	You must have an empty factory somewhere!
ACCOMMODTN OFFICER	No, you look. I've got thousands of homeless bloody people up there walking around and I've got enough on with them without being worried about bloody criminals.
CHIEF SUPERINTNDT	Well, you're gonna have to find somewhere to put 'em aren't you?
ACCOMMODTN OFFICER	Well, I don't know. Look, shoot the buggers. I don't care.

The CHIEF SUPERINTENDENT *walks off before they come to blows. The* INFORMATION OFFICER *comes across and hands a piece of paper to the* ACCOMMODATION OFFICER.

ACCOMMODTN OFFICER	Oh, Christ, Steve. This should have been sorted out days ago. Here...

INFORMATION OFFICER: What about rest centres? Can we not tell them to make their way there?

ACCOMMODTN OFFICER: No. No. There's no point. They're overrun anyway.

INFORMATION OFFICER: What about tents? Are there any tents we could have?

ACCOMMODTN OFFICER: Tents! How the hell should I know? Look, if you want to know about tents, phone the bloody Boy Scouts.

INFORMATION OFFICER: Oh piss off, will you! You're not the only one under pressure.

ACCOMMODTN OFFICER: I bloody know!

CHIEF SUPERINTNDT: *(on the radio)* ... and what the hell are you doing about digging us out, that's what I'd like to know?

97. Documentary footage.

A shot of devastation.

Caption: 'Friday June 17th. Attack plus twenty-two days'.

98. Documentary footage.

Dirty, poor-looking rats among the ruins of buildings.

Caption: 'Likely Epidemics: Cholera, Dysentry. Typhoid'.

99. Interior. Becketts' house. Day.

The slippered feet of GRANNY *are glimpsed in the wreckage of the Beckett house. A dog sniffs around the body, then is frightened away by a noise. Three looters emerge from the cellar.*

LOOTER: Bloody hell, what a stink! Let's get out of here before I puke.

100. Exterior. Becketts' house. Day.

THE LOOTERS *come out into the ruins and start examining their loot.*

SOLDIER Halt, or I fire!

ONE OF THE LOOTERS *starts to run.*

OFFICER Number three. A round at that man over there.

The SOLDIER *shoots and the man falls to the ground.*

OFFICER Number one—go and search the house.

ONE OF THE SOLDIERS *goes into the house. The* OFFICER *and* ANOTHER SOLDIER *spreadeagle* THE LOOTERS *against the wall.*

OFFICER Don't you know the penalty for looting?

LOOTERS I ain't looting... that's not looting, searching an empty house.. what choice have we got? What else can we do? We're starving.

The soldier returns from inside the house.

SOLDIER Two bodies in the cellar, sir, Man and woman. They've not been dead long. The man's had his head battered in.

LOOTER It weren't us. It were him. We ain't done nothing.

They are led away.

OFFICER Have you got the stolen goods? Search the house, then the body.

Two soldiers stay behind to carry out the orders.

SOLDIER 1 Packet of crisps.

SOLDIER 2 What flavour are they?

SOLDIER 1 Prawn cocktail.

SOLDIER 2 They fucking would be. I hate them. Come on.

THE SOLDIERS *move away and leave the body.*

101. Interior. Becketts' house. Day.

The dog has returned to sniff and scavenge around GRANNY BECKETT's *body.*

102. Documentary footage.

Scenes of devastation and ramshackle homes. People stand with ragged clothes.

RADIO VOICE All able-bodied citizens, men, women and children, should report for reconstruction duties commencing 0800 hours tomorrow morning. The inhabitants of Release Band A—that is Dore and Totley, Abbeydale and Woodseats—should rendezvous in Abbeydale Park. Release Band B...

People are queueing for food and stuffing it into their mouths.

COMMENTARY Money has had no meaning since the attack. The only viable currency is food given as reward for work or withheld as punishment. In the grim economics of the aftermath, there are two harsh realities. A survivor who can work gets more food than one who can't, and the more who die, the more food is left for the rest.

103. Exterior. Graveyard. Day.

MR KEMP, *very ill, is sitting up against a gravestone in a feeding centre which has been set up in the graveyard. People are eating a meagre ration of thin stew and bread. A* MAN *next to him speaks to him without looking.*

MAN I could murder a fag now. I used to love a fag after a meal.

MR KEMP Have you got owt to swap?

MAN I've got some scotch.

MR KEMP *slowly produces a packet of cigarettes and hands them over to the man. He receives the scotch in return.*

104. Exterior. Graveyard. Night.

> MR KEMP *is drunk. He is sitting in the same place in the graveyard, lit by the flames of the fire. He takes a swig of scotch but immediately retches and is sick. He has been playing with* MICHAEL'*s battery game, and we hear the noise that it makes.*

105. Exterior. Footage of dead bodies.

> *Pictures of dead bodies, among them* MR KEMP'*s.*
>
> *Caption: 'Disposal of bodies: no spare fuel for cremation. No spare fuel for bulldozers. Wasteful of manpower to dig pits by hand. Unburied corpses in U.K. estimated ten to twenty million.*

106. Exterior. Tennis club. Day.

> *A guard is on duty at the gates. Lots of people are behind the wire fences. A Traffic Warden is patrolling.*
>
> *Caption: 'Dore and Totley Tennis Club. Attack plus four weeks'.*

COMMENTARY Detention camps are improvised to cope with looters. Their numbers are growing.

LOOTER ... I'm buggered if I'm going to be shot by a Traffic Warden...

107. Interior. Bunker.

> *The bunker is pitch black. Torch lights are being shone down through the entrance as the search party arrives.*

VOICE Watch yourselves here, lads... Put that light down here...

> *The light picks up the* CHIEF SUPERINTENDENT *lying at his desk. His face is grey with death. It is the same with* MR SUTTON *and the rest.*

108. Interior. Becketts' house. Day.

The dead body of GRANNY *is still lying in the room. Rats are running all over it.* RUTH *enters the room, peers into the cellar, then turns and leaves the house. She does not show any emotion.*

109. Interior. A squash court. Day.

Caption: 'Special courts of justice given wide-ranging powers'.

The back wall of the squash court is splattered with blood and bullet holes. One LOOTER *is sitting on a stool against the wall; a second is having his shirt taken off by a soldier. A shot rings out and the first* LOOTER *falls off the stool, dead.*

110. Documentary still.

A shot of a devastated building.

Caption: 'Five weeks after attack'.

Cut to shot of RUTH.

Caption: 'No electricity. No mains water. No sanitation'.

Caption: 'Fuel stocks: diminishing. Transport: difficult. Food supplies: unreliable'.

111. Exterior. Moorland. Day.

A long line of stragglers make their way across the land. Some fall on the hard ground and do not get up again. Many are sick and injured, and all carry their last few possessions. Among them is RUTH.

COMMENTARY A growing exodus from cities in search of food. It's July. The countryside is cold and full of unknown radiation hazards. By now, five to six weeks after the attack, deaths from the effects of fallout are approaching their peak.

RUTH, *now visibly pregnant, finds a puddle of water and*

gets down on the ground to smash the ice which covers it. She hesitates for a moment, and then drinks.

The refugees trudge on.

RUTH *glances around and furtively takes out a can of processed peas. She proceeds to smash it on the rock.*

Overhead a small plane circles.

VOICE FROM PLANE Return to your homes. Return to your homes. Return to your homes. Return to your homes. Turn back. Turn back...

The refugees angrily stop walking to shout abuse and shake their fists at the plane. RUTH *looks up but does not shout. Hungrily, she eats the contents of the tin she has managed to open.*

112. Exterior. Buxton. Day.

Caption: 'Buxton. Twenty miles from Sheffield'.

Buxton town centre has been undamaged by the blast but is overrun by refugees from Sheffield and Manchester.

POLICEMAN Right down there.

RUTH *and a crowd of refugees are walking along a backstreet of small terraced houses with* TWO POLICEMEN. ONE OF THE POLICEMEN *approaches a house and bangs on the door, which opens a fraction.*

POLICEMAN George Langley?

LANGLEY What do you want?

POLICEMAN You've been designated four temporary residents.

LANGLEY I'm not having no strangers live here.

POLICEMAN Look, you've got no choice in the matter. It's law under the new Emergency regulations.

LANGLEY I don't care what it is. This is my house and I'm having no strangers here.

POLICEMAN Look, according to my records you've got four spare rooms, kitchen, bathroom...

LANGLEY Aye, and they're stopping spare an' all... You can't just walk into peoples' houses. It's not right.

POLICEMAN Look, we're not here to argue the rights and wrongs of the matter. Right, you four. One, two, three, four. Come on—in you go. Come on.

RUTH is one of the four counted in to Langley's house.

LANGLEY Besides, it might be bloody dangerous. They might bring all sorts of diseases with them. They might be contaminated. Look at him.

POLICEMAN Right. Number nineteen.

Langley continues to mutter and curse to himself about the matter.

113. Exterior. Langley's street. Day.

A paper bag hits the ground and its contents scatter all over the place. A shotgun is heard.

LANGLEY Get out, will you... the whole lot of you!

RUTH rushes over to the bag and quickly picks up the last few possessions she has. All the other refugees are being pushed out of the Langley house too.

EVICTED REFUGEES Where can we go? We're supposed to stay here. We're billeted with you. You've no right to chuck us out. Police said we were to stay here. Miserable old git. We've nowhere else to go. Where're we supposed to go?

114. Exterior. Food camp. Day.

REFUGEES are eating a meagre meal of bread and soup. RUTH is among them, sitting on her own.

VOICE This is a final warning. Residents and non-residents must register at the Town Hall for I.D. cards and ration tickets. No provisions will be issued to anyone without them.

Feeding will now be on alternate days. Numbers one to five hundred will be fed today, the remainder tomorrow.

A man walks into shot and sits down beside RUTH. *It is* BOB—*Jimmy's workmate.*

BOB Ruth? It is Ruth isn't it?

RUTH *does not acknowledge* BOB *at all, and carries on eating.*

BOB I'm Bob, Jimmy's mate. We met once or twice, remember? You came to our last Christmas do at work... Where is he? Is he with you? Have you seen him?

RUTH *still does not communicate with* BOB.

115. Exterior. Moorland. Day.

Caption: 'Six weeks after attack'.

On a frozen moorland BOB *and* RUTH *are looking at a dead sheep.*

RUTH Is it safe to eat?

BOB How can you tell? It's got a thick coat. That should have protected it.

RUTH You breathe it in, though, don't you?

BOB It should be alright.

He takes out a knife.

RUTH Sheep don't die of cold. It must be radiation.

BOB You'd be able to taste it if it were contaminated.

RUTH I don't know.

BOB Anyway, we've no choice, have we? Unless we want to starve to death.

RUTH *scrambles down to* BOB, *who begins to cut away at the sheep. They eat hungrily at the raw meat.*

116. Exterior. Moorland. Day.

BOB   I think I'll take some with me.

RUTH   Where?

BOB   City.

RUTH   There's nothing there.

BOB   North. Dales... it doesn't really matter, does it? It's all the same... Try and skin it—keep me warm.

He goes to the sheep to investigate the possibilities of skinning it, while RUTH *continues to eat.*

117. Exterior. Countryside.

Still shot of a shanty town.

Caption: 'September. Four months after attack'.

RUTH *is asleep in a farm outbuilding. As she dreams, images come to her of* JIMMY *in his aviary and a baby in a pushchair. She opens her eyes suddenly, and closes them again.*

Caption: 'Direct effects of attack: deaths between seventeen and thirty-eight million from blast, heat and fallout. Remaining population weak, cold and hungry'.

VOICE BROADCASTING   If we are to survive these difficult early months and establish a firm base for the re-development of our country, then we must concentrate all our energies on agricultural production.

Still shot of a barren landscape.

118. Still footage. Countryside.

Still shots of damaged crops.

Caption: 'Attack in Spring: darkness and cold reduce plant activity to very low levels. Little ripening of crops'.

Still shots of dead sheep and cattle.

119. Exterior. Countryside. Day.

A group of men and women, looking exhausted and underfed, are working a field in the barren landscape. RUTH *is among them. Combines are being used to gather the corn. Some of the workers are seriously ill and finding it difficult to work.*

COMMENTARY Collecting this diminishing first harvest is now—literally—a matter of life and death.

Someone falls to the ground, unable to go on.

120. Interior. Barn. Day.

A threshing machine stands in the barn. A soldier stands watching the pouring of petrol.

COMMENTARY Chronic fuel shortages mean that this could be one of the last times tractors and combine harvesters are used in Britain.

In the foreground A WOMAN *shovels grain into a sack held open by* ANOTHER WOMAN. *The all work in silence.*

121. Exterior. Farm buildings. Day.

It is a cold, bitter day. RUTH *struggles across the skyline towards some farm buildings, stumbling on the rough ground. Her pregnancy is very far advanced, and she clutches her stomach.*

Caption: 'Exposure to radiation in early pregnancy: foetus carries high risk of deformity and mental retardation'.

As RUTH *enters the farmyard, a dog barks at her ferociously. Although it is on a chain, it will not let her pass. She rushes into an outbuilding and lies down in the straw.*

She delivers the baby herself. All the while, outside, the dog is barking and growling.

The BABY *cries out, and* RUTH *sees that it is physically normal. She cries, and holds the baby to her.*

122. Interior. Barn. Night.

Caption: 'Sunday December 25th'.

A forlorn group of refugees are sitting around a fire in a barn. Many of them are injured, and suffering from burns. RUTH's BABY *is crying, but then stops, leaving complete quiet apart from the crackling of the fire.*

123. Exterior. Moorland.

Bodies are lying frozen in the snow.

COMMENTARY The first winter. The stresses of hypothermia, epidemic and radiation fall heavily on the very young and the old—their protective layers of flesh are thinner. In the first few winters, many of the young and old disappear from Britain.

124. Grain supplies.

Caption: 'March, ten months after attack'.

A SOLDIER *is guarding grain in a sack.*

125. Exterior. An alley in Buxton. Day.

RUTH *runs frantically down an alley, clutching her baby and some grain she has just stolen. In the background there is shouting and the sounds of shots being fired. A helicopter circles above, causing a terrific wind.*

VOICE FROM HELICOPTER Halt. . . halt! If you do not halt we will open fire. Halt at once!

Some of the grain is on the ground, being scattered by the wind. RUTH *keeps on running.*

126. Interior. Barn. Day.

RUTH *almost weeping, is crushing the grain she has stolen to get out the flour. The* BABY *waits patiently, wrapped in a rough blanket.* RUTH *blows the grain to separate the chaff.*

Cuts to stills of devastation.

127. Exterior. Street in Buxton. Day.

Caption: 'May. One year after attack'.

First we see more stills of devastation. Then a street in Buxton, with people carrying their possessions, or pulling prams and carts with their 'homes' in them. RUTH *is standing talking to a* DIRTY MAN *who is sitting with a large basket in front of a huge billboard which displays an insurance poster. She is bartering with him, pushing away others who come up and try to do the same.* THE MAN *does not respond as she offers him her last few things, but then he gets up and whispers something into* RUTH'S *ear; she nods her head and stares at him.*

We see that inside THE MAN'S *basket is a pile of dead rats. He puts three into Ruth's old carrier bag.*

128. Documentary footage.

The sky.

Caption: 'Skies become clearer. Returning sunlight now heavier with ultra-violet light'.

In a barren field people are working by hand. They have cloth covering their faces. Their hoes are trying to make an impression on the hard ground.

Caption: 'Cataracts widespread. Higher risk of cancers and leukaemias. Second and subsequent harvests: no fertilisers, no agrochemicals. Crops susceptible to viruses, disease and insects'.

We see flies buzzing about, and maggots on a decaying body.

Caption: 'Three to eight years after attack population reaches minimum. U.K. numbers may decline to mediaeval levels. Possibly between four and eleven million'.

Cut to shot of dead man in a field.

129. Exterior. Field. Day.

Caption: 'Ten years after. Ruth and her daughter'.

People are working the field with hand-held hoes. Someone falls to the ground and we see that it is RUTH. *She looks old and ill. Someone walks over to her:* JANE, *her daughter. Although she looks normal, she is slightly mentally retarded. She looks down without emotion at* RUTH *lying on the ground in the barren landscape.*

130. Interior. Barn. Day.

RUTH *is on a rough bed, asleep.* JANE *stands by her. She shakes* RUTH.

JANE   Ruth. Ruth. Work. Work. Up.

JANE's *speech is unformed and ungrammatical.*

RUTH *does not respond for some time. When she eventually opens her eyes it is just for a moment. She holds out her hand to* JANE, *who takes it. Then* RUTH *closes her eyes. She is dead.*

JANE *shows no emotion at finding that she cannot rouse her mother. She looks under* RUTH's *pillow and takes out a hairbrush and one or two of Ruth's last remaining possessions. The bird book of* JIMMY's *(which Ruth has had all this time) has no meaning for Jane. She leaves it behind.*

131. Interior. Large Room.

A television screen is showing a video of an old schools' programme. The picture is very distorted.

SCHOOLS'   'Words... and... pictures'. Skeletons and skulls of different
BROADCAST creatures.

We borrowed them from the Museum. Did you recognize what some of the skeletons were?

A group of children are watching the programme with dumb-looking faces. The video recorder is covered in dust.

			It works off a single cable hanging from the ceiling.

SCHOOLS' BROADCAST   There was the skeleton of a cat—a cat's skeleton. The skeleton of a chicken—a chicken's skeleton. The skeleton of a bird—a bird's skeleton.

All this means nothing to the children, who sit in silence. An OLD WOMAN *is with the children, and she mouths the words as the presenter says them. We see that* JANE *is among the group.*

132. Interior. Shed. Day.

The shed has been converted into a workroom. Water drips through the ceiling. Children sit round tables, unpicking thread and wool from old garments, once more in the charge of the OLD WOMAN, *who is asleep.* JANE *concentrates intently on her work.*

133. Exterior. Landscape. Day.

A devastated landscape. People search through ruins for scrap metal. Men work at the coal seam with hand picks. We see a few steam traction engines.

Caption: 'Thirteen years after'.

134. Interior. Farm buiding.

In a desolate farm building, JANE *is tending a fire. A dead rabbit lies beside her.* TWO YOUNG MEN *enter the barn, and* JANE *picks up the rabbit and holds it behind her back. In her other hand she has a stick which she brandishes at the* TWO YOUNG MEN. *The speak to her in a language which is difficult to understand.*

SPIKE Hoy! What'n be? *(Meaning: 'What is it?')*

GAZ Seed'n. N'coney. *(Meaning: 'I saw it. It's a rabbit.')*

SPIKE Giss'n. Come on. Giss'n. *(Meaning: 'Give it to us.')*

GAZ Better, else us'll bray'n. *(Meaning: 'You better had. Or else we'll beat you.')*

JANE *looks frightened but defiant.*

JANE Best stand off 'fore tha'll ger'n. *(Meaning: 'You'd better stand back or else you'll get hit.')*

GAZ Where'n stop at? Come'n us? *(Meaning: 'Where are you staying? Are you coming with us?')*

JANE Where'n?

GAZ Us place. Gaz 'n Spike.

SPIKE Share'n coney, then. Come an' share'n coney. Giss'n. *(Meaning: 'Share the rabbit with us, then. Give it here')*

135. Exterior. Street in Buxton. Day.

JANE, GAZ *and* SPIKE *are running through the ruins with a bag of loot.*

VOICE Hey, you! Come back here with that!

Shots are fired and GAZ *falls dead.* JANE *and* SPIKE *carry on undeterred. We see them running across the skyline to the deserted farm buildings.*

136. Interior. Old farm building

JANE *and* SPIKE *dive down into the straw and open their bag of loot.* JANE *snatches at a loaf of bread.*

SPIKE Giss'n. Come on. Giss'n.

He grabs at it and they begin to play around. Their wrestling turns sexual, and we hear JANE *exclaiming as they have crude intercourse.*

Cut to a series of various stills; a refugee huddled in a corner; a soldier hanging his head; a man injured by the Hiroshima bomb; an old man on a bed; a devastated landscape.

137. Exterior. Buxton. Night.

It is nine months later and JANE, *very pregnant, is walking through the streets of Buxton. As she staggers over the rubble, she passes a ramshackle house. A door is opened and we see the light inside and hear a short burst of music—the same song that was on the car radio at the very beginning.*

JANE *passes bodies hanging from a gallows. There is an atmosphere of tension and* JANE *is frightened.*

SOLDIER Halt! Halt!

Shots are fired.

138. Interior. Hospital. Night.

JANE *enters the hospital. She is in urgent need of attention. Nobody shows any concern. She goes up to* A WOMAN *who seems to be in charge. The* WOMAN *takes no notice at first and carries on making the beds.*

WOMAN What's wrong, have you been hurt?

JANE Babby. N'come. Coming.

WOMAN Oh, no time for babbies here. No time for babbies. You'll have to go home and use your commonsense.

JANE *is now in pain and grabs at the* WOMAN *and a bed.*

JANE N'coming! N'coming!

139. Interior. Hospital. Night.

The baby is delivered in the hospital. JANE *is in a bed and crying out when the pain is bad. Other patients take no notice of her. The baby is being wrapped in a bloody cloth which it has just been wiped with. There is silence. The baby is given to* JANE, *who stares down at the bundle in her arms. Her face turns to horror and disgust. She pushes the baby away from her and opens her mouth to scream.*

Freeze frame.

Roll end credits.